T0280192

The Secrets
of
Successful
Relationships

Published in 2024 by The School of Life
First published in the USA in 2024
930 High Road, London, N12 9RT

Copyright © The School of Life 2024

Designed and typeset by @marciamihotichstudio
Printed in Latvia by Livonia Print

All rights reserved. This book is sold subject to the condition that
it shall not be resold, lent, hired out or otherwise circulated without
express prior consent of the publisher.

A proportion of this book has appeared online at
www.theschooloflife.com/articles

Every effort has been made to contact the copyright holders of the
material reproduced in this book. If any have been inadvertently
overlooked, the publisher will be pleased to make restitution at the
earliest opportunity.

The School of Life publishes a range of books on essential topics in
psychological and emotional life, including relationships, parenting,
friendship, careers and fulfilment. The aim is always to help us
to understand ourselves better – and thereby to grow calmer, less
confused and more purposeful. Discover our full range of titles,
including books for children, here:
www.theschooloflife.com/books

The School of Life also offers a comprehensive therapy service,
which complements, and draws upon, our published works:
www.theschooloflife.com/therapy

www.theschooloflife.com

ISBN 978-1-916753-01-3

10 9 8 7 6 5 4 3 2 1

p. 86 Photo by Metin Ozer on Unsplash

The Secrets
of
Successful
Relationships

The School of Life

Contents

Introduction

A melancholy paradox lies at the heart of modern relationships: practically everyone on Earth longs to be loved and to love within stable, long-term, flourishing couples, but, on the ground, contented unions are dauntingly rare. We have ourselves probably been looking for rewarding love for a long time already; we may have been on a succession of awkward dates and met a number of people who seemed delightful at first; we may have lived with someone for a while; we might even have been married. But, of course, nothing has worked out. That is why we are here. The questions go on.

What we can be sure of from the outset is that, whatever society sometimes implies, the problem does not lie with us alone. We need not compound our misery by thinking it unique. If we were magically given wings, we might skim over any large modern city and look down at a range of newly formed couples: one pair might be holding hands in a fashionable bar, another would be lazing together in bed, a third would be flirting at work – all would be feeling excited and blessed. But we would need only skip forward a few years for the overall picture to grow darker.

7

The majority of couples would have separated (some would have forgotten each other's names). Only a small number would have married and, of these, a fair few would have divorced in acrimony. Some would be sticking together mainly for the sake of a child or because they could not afford to split. Only a tiny number would be beaming at us and confiding that their wishes had largely been honoured. The world encourages us to place our faith in a kind of love that, on the basis of the predominant evidence, seems barely to exist.

Are we being tricked? Why do so few couples succeed? It is tempting to believe that those who work out have been granted a form of divine favour. But we cannot build a decent life on the hope of randomly distributed heavenly munificence. Is there anything we can do in our search for sound intimate lives other than offer libations to the gods?

The premise of the argument here is that there is no need for superstition or despair. Good relationships are neither mysterious nor random. There are solid, rationally structured explanations for why some people do well together while others – despite powerful initial hopes and touchingly idealistic intentions – do not. Success only seems random because we have, to date, operated with an insufficiently firm grip on the actual mechanics of true love.

There are, in reality, only a small number of fundamental factors that account for the well-being of every robust, loving couple. Though relationships might seem infinitely varied, whether they succeed or fail comes down, in essence, to the presence – or absence – of a handful of emotional skills. Stated briefly, the five anchors of successful relationships are:

i.   A mutual, nondefensive readiness to admit to imperfections.
ii.   A willingness to let ourselves be vulnerable.
iii.   A generous, compassionate response to our flaws and errors.
iv.   A therapeutic reaction to what is 'mad' inside both of us.
v.   A sufficient lack of anger to keep admiration alive.

The list may sound simple. As we will see, enacting it is the work of a lifetime. Nevertheless, if these psychological ingredients are reliably – and mutually – in place, then the normal trials and stresses of coupledom can be both faced and survived, just as if these qualities are absent, no other advantage will ever manage to fend off eventual collapse.

It is striking how different these anchors of love are to the qualities we're typically encouraged to trust in when considering the sources of romantic happiness. There is no reference here to looks, money, shared hobbies, a similar taste in films or, indeed, 'chemistry'. It is not that any of these factors (routinely cited in wedding speeches) are undesirable. They are plainly extremely helpful and at certain points compelling; they are just never decisive. That two people have good careers, both like rollerblading and once felt delighted to be together as an August sun went down over the terracotta roofs of a Mediterranean coastal town ultimately tells us very little about their chances of enduring together the unavoidable maelstroms of existence.

The real issue is how two individuals who are necessarily radically imperfect at their core might stay united – and thrive – without giving way to fury, boredom, despair or bitterness. And it's to this question that our five emotional anchors offer solutions. They present us with the psychological wherewithal for dealing with what is most knotty and gnarled in ourselves and our partners, and for navigating the frustrations and incompatibilities that no wedding speech will ever allude to but that will in time eat away at our sweetest hopes and most sincere plans.

Ultimately every relationship is a meeting between two shockingly complicated people and their tortuous and only half-understood histories. The qualities that help us in this encounter are those that enable us to fathom, withstand, forgive, harmonise and laugh over our differences. Compatibility is an achievement of love; it should never be a precondition.

Though we may look at the list of emotional qualities and feel initially dismayed at all that we lack, we can be assured that emotional maturation is possible. Love is – in the end – a skill, not an emotion. Successful relationships are a special kind of achievement. Their inner workings are comprehensible and attainable. We don't have to be locked into a cycle of enthusiasm followed by sadness. With the appropriate prompts and careful assistance, we can take the first steps towards the kind of fulfilling, long-term union that we have for so long aspired to and deserve. We can – though our culture makes the idea sound unfairly strange – *learn* to love.

1.

The Five Anchors of Love

We have mentioned five attitudes that anchor love. What do these actually involve? And how can we hope to cultivate these attitudes in ourselves and our partners in order that affection can flourish and endure?

(i) Nondefensiveness

An ingrained tendency

One of the most basic features of our natures is that we are defensive. That is, we seek to ward off psychic pain and defend ourselves against perceived attacks. Our minds are squeamish. We try to uphold a bearable picture of ourselves in the face of any possible insights or criticisms that others may direct towards us (or that could emanate from the more perceptive recesses of our own minds). We are not keen on feedback. Our defensiveness is a profoundly understandable tendency. And yet it is also behind a predominant share of the failure of all relationships.

However sweet and fascinating two people might initially be, it is inescapable that they will also, with time and the birth of true intimacy, stumble upon aspects of one another's characters that cannot help but generate difficulties and a degree of dismay. Each partner could be determined to be only kind, but the way that they shell an egg, leave the bathroom, deal with their suitcase on returning from a trip, handle the household keys or tell an anecdote will gradually unleash powerful degrees of frustration or puzzlement in those they must share their lives with.

The problem starts when we, as partners, venture to air how we feel. We might start out politely and tentatively. We may gently mention the strands of hair in the basin or the muddled telling of anecdotes in front of strangers. But thoughtful receptivity can be hard to come by. Our partner is in danger of treating our remarks as if they were a direct attack, not as comments about something a sound adult could ever really be bothered by; they might go strangely quiet or immediately accuse us of being hugely unkind or malevolently judgemental. Or they might slyly turn the tables and start listing – with less and less good humour – certain things that they find awful about us and that they have been holding on to privately for a long time. Whatever strategy they adopt, the underlying meaning tends to be the same: that being found in some way imperfect is entirely unacceptable and deeply contrary to the spirit of true love.

'Love me for who I am' is the fateful rallying cry of all lovers headed for disaster; it is in reality a monstrously unfair (though entirely understandable) demand to be loved just as we are, with all our panoply of faults, compulsions and immaturities. But with a modicum of self-awareness and honesty, we should only ever expect to be loved for who we hope to be, for who we are in our best moments, for the good that lies in us in a latent and yet not-realised state.

The spirit of true love should require that whenever there is feedback, we turn gratefully to our partner and ask for more, that we continuously search to access a better version of ourselves, that we see love as a classroom in which our lover can teach us one or two things about who we should become – rather than as a burrow in which our existing errors can be sentimentally endorsed and encouraged.

Where defensiveness comes from

In order to overcome defensiveness, we need to understand its sources; we have to think about defensiveness not in its obdurate, dismaying present manifestations but in its greatly more benevolent and engaging origins. Defensiveness is almost invariably founded on an intimate history that no defensive person consciously chose and that – compassionately recounted – might move us to tears. Defensiveness is a legacy of early pain. There might have been a shy 6-year-old with a robust, confident parent who was ashamed of their timid, lonely child. No one much seemed to care for this soft-cheeked, large-eyed creature at home. There were criticisms and hints that another sibling was favoured. Love, as this poor soul encountered it, was a scarce, easily lost commodity. For anything to be pointed out to them was (as they came to think) a harbinger of fresh contempt and renewed exclusion from everything sustaining and kind. Or else a parent was intermittently admiring and then terrifyingly angry at their offspring if there was the slightest drop in their performance at school.

Defensive people did not magically acquire their ferocity in relation to our comments; they suffered some form of early neglect or encounter with unsteady, fluctuating warmth. No wonder such a person might respond with alarm, even viciousness, when the slightest negative thought about them rears its head in a lover they felt ready to entrust with their whole being. There could – in the mind of the unfortunate sufferer – plainly be no such thing as affectionate criticism, no such thing as helpful feedback, no possibility of being at once adored and upbraided. Love cannot be conceived of as coexisting alongside occasional moments of evaluation. It is on the basis of such awkward, emotionally scarred internal associations that defensiveness is built.

Unwinding defensiveness

A less-defended attitude isn't a random gift; it is something we can aim for, every bit as much as we can aim for a flatter stomach or a tidier house. Even if we didn't have an ideal introduction to life, we can access ideas that dismantle the equation between love-worthiness and untouchable perfection. We can begin to become less defensive when we take some of the following ideas on board:

Our early experience isn't a guide to the present: Our defences were the best we could do in the face of early harshness. We were confronted with problems and demands far beyond our strength. But a decent partner, if we let them know our background troubles, will be moved by our tender desperation and hasty fear. And they can, so long as we master our panic, help us to see that the thing we should be afraid of now is not criticism but an inability to accept its occasional kindly manifestations.

By the background standard of the defensive person, no one could ever be loved: If love really required an absence of even the most minor flaws, no one could possibly qualify for a relationship. Yet, in reality, we are love-worthy not because we are perfect but because none of us ever can be.

Irritation isn't objective: We need not feel overly targeted by criticism. Every partner has their own particular fixations and preoccupations that mean they will latch on to certain features of another's character. That a partner is annoyed with us over something is no sign that we are doing anything appalling per se, and so we can afford to feel unpersecuted by their judgement. Some people wouldn't mind a messy cupboard; not everyone cares about a lengthy anecdote. An issue can be worth discussing amicably not because it is a fundamental failing but simply because it happens to bother someone we love.

Love isn't fragile: In the defensive person's mind, the smallest comment is like the small rockfall that announces an avalanche. There seems to be no way to trust that it really is just about how long pasta should be cooked for, or the right way to make a bed – the underlying intention seems always to be to inflict a devastating wound and speed the entire relationship to a close. The defensive person has not had a chance to experience the robustness of love; how it is wholly possible to call someone the worst names in the lexicon and then, ten minutes later, want to lie softly in their arms, tenderness having been renewed and reinvigorated by an opportunity to purge frustration. There can be ruptures – and repair. True love is resilient; it is not destroyed by a detail but only ever by the way that a detail can't be acknowledged or processed.

Defensiveness can be outgrown. We can learn to measure in our hearts the difference between a complaint and an existential rejection; we can come to hear a criticism without connecting it to damnation. That love once seemed fragile doesn't mean it must be today. We can trust that we may on occasion irritate a partner without concluding that they will therefore hate everything about us into eternity.

When searching for a partner, we need to look out for someone who can join us in the noble quest to recognise and overcome defensiveness. We might even raise this ambition on an early date ('I'd like one day to move to the country, learn Spanish and, with a lover's help, get over my defensiveness,' we might declare by way of introduction to our goals). We could frame the attempt to listen to criticism without fury or hurt as one of life's mightiest challenges – alongside sporting excellence or business success. Eventually, with a lot of effort, we would hope to reach a stage when a partner could point out with tact and humanity that we had bad breath or that our shoes didn't match our jumper and, rather than reacting as we have grown up to do, we could simply turn to them, smile benignly and say what flawed humans should always respond with when another member of the species deigns to help them to grow into a better version of themselves: 'Thank you.'

(ii) Vulnerability

There's a second crucial criterion for relationship success: the person who is good at love is good at being vulnerable.

What is vulnerability?

We make ourselves psychologically vulnerable whenever we let a partner know some of the ways in which we are weak, needy, scared, immature, incompetent or just plain odd – that is, some of the ways in which we are human. To be vulnerable is to dare to take off the usual cloak of normality and sensibleness with which we navigate the world and, for once, to show someone who we really are, with all the fragility and unusualness implied. We might, as vulnerable people, admit to desiring to be mummied or daddied, to curling into a ball late at night, to crying over so-called small things, to harbouring a distinctive fetish, to wanting to call up our lover every ten minutes, to suffering from anxiety and paranoia, to liking to speak in regressive voices and to having a favourite toy called Yellow Bear.

Why vulnerability is a risk

It's a hugely complicated step to confess – especially in front of someone we fundamentally want to impress and secure the affection of – that there are basic ways in which we fall short of what a proper adult is meant to be like. A certain kind of no-nonsense partner might well tell us sternly to grow up, complain about us to their friends and make hasty moves to end the relationship.

As a result, we often lie, not for advantage or thievery, but in order to hold on to a love we desperately want to rely on. We pretend to be strong and unafraid. We disown our needs and longings. We put on a show of being someone else. Such acting works in many contexts. An uncomplaining, breezy competence and unemotive intelligence probably makes for an ideal employee, an admirable committee member and a thoroughly respectable citizen of the modern world.

But in an intimate relationship, this form of barricaded caution is fatal. Our fears and inadequacies don't vanish because we have hidden them; we don't get any less child-like or odd because we have learnt to seem sensible. We simply end up making it impossible for a partner to know us – and, because they are likely to take their lead from our own reserve, they will be unable to show themselves to us in turn. We enclose ourselves in the high walls of our deceptions.

The heroism of vulnerability

To dare to be vulnerable involves a faith that whatever we are inwardly most afraid and ashamed of in our own natures must have counterparts in other people. We cannot be alone in our oddities. The only people we can assume are 'normal' are those we don't yet know very well. But once we are past the flawless exterior, every person we meet – and especially the person we are now dating – will have their share of follies and tender spots: they will fart, suck their thumbs, be scared of ghosts, have psychological compulsions and worry about the size of their ears or the state of their friendships. We are guaranteed not to be alone in our fear and neediness. And what is more, it's only on the basis of mutual disclosure of susceptibility that a true bond can be built. We may admire paragons of strength and stoicism; we can never properly love them.

To be vulnerable is in essence to let a partner catch sight of a side of us that dates back to childhood: the distant time when we feared Mummy would never come back, when we cried and no one comforted us, when Daddy shouted at us and we were frozen with terror, when a rough friend told us we were a baby for still loving our stuffed elephant, when no one wanted to play with us at school, when we tried and tried to explain but Granny was still angry. To be properly, fully vulnerable is to take the other into the frightened, small places of our past and to let them see that we're still in significant ways the little, distressed people we once were. Honest, vibrant love is an encounter between two vulnerable children who otherwise do a very good job of masquerading as adults.

Why we flee from our own vulnerability

What makes people reject the offer of vulnerability? The strength they insist on displaying to the world is an indicator of how punishing they have had to be towards their fragile inner selves; it's a measure of how fast they have had to grow up. If Mummy dismissed their night-time fears, they will have had to try to tell themselves – desperately – that Mummy was right and that cry-babies really are disgusting. They perhaps deflected the rough boys' taunting of Minko (who Granny knitted while they were still in the womb and whose trunk had half disintegrated under the intensity of their hugs) by throwing the little soft toy in the bin. They managed their traumas by siding with those who hurt them. They focused on keeping their room tidy, passing exams and learning how to do business. And so they came to fear the very thing that they now most need: an enfolding, restorative and profoundly understanding tenderness towards their traumatised early selves. In a grim paradox, to have words of empathy whispered to them lovingly in the dark only reinforces their deepest fears; their protective shell snaps ever more tightly shut at the approach of sympathetic love; they respond to their own needs with panic and self-disgust.

Learning vulnerability

We learn to be vulnerable by understanding that those who conveyed the imperative of a tougher (noncrying, nonfragile) self were profoundly incorrect and, in their way, deeply traumatised themselves. Mummy was dismissive of our fears not because she was impressively astute in her theories of human development but because she was struggling with her own history of unattended need. The anti-Minko 'friend' wasn't showing us the real path to being a grown-up; they were inflicting on us some of the unkindness that had in other contexts been directed at them. We need to go back and convince ourselves – perhaps with a touch of anger – of how misguided the agents of our 'growing up' really were.

Finding a partner with whom we can be vulnerable constitutes a supreme act of restoration. After a lifetime of denial and false strength, we stand to find in another the sympathy that was sorely needed, but unavailable to us, in the past. The old wounds can be gently tended; we become stronger by learning to speak the language of weakness. By letting our hurt, babyish selves into the relationship, we open the way to a more nuanced, fruitful, creative and accurate way of being an adult.

(iii) Tenderness

Love has a third important – but not always easily recognised – ingredient: tenderness. Tenderness often gets overlooked because what it really involves is compassion at a very particular moment: *the moment when compassion isn't obviously deserved.* Relationships succeed when it is a partner's less edifying and unworthy behaviours that remain capable of arousing, alongside a deep sigh, doses of unearned redemptive empathy.

Why we're not tender

In theory, we all have plenty of time for compassion, but we tend to have some specific notions of where and when this quality should really be deployed. We typically reserve it for the most obviously blameless candidates: those who are sad but entirely good, those who have lost their livelihoods through no fault of their own, those who were born into unfortunate circumstances, struck by lightning or rendered homeless by earthquakes.

What we find it much harder to do is to forgive someone who appears to be behaving suboptimally on purpose, who seems to have made an active choice to mess things up, who looks as if they have taken a negative path out of wilfulness, idiocy or nastiness; someone who had options to be successful or respectable, calm or grown up, but instead – for reasons we have no energy to investigate – decided to shout, to be mean, to respond ungratefully or to display immaturity. We know we are kind people, but we surely cannot be expected to love where love is undeserved.

The true nature of love

And yet that is exactly where love should and must be deployed if relationships are to survive. True love cannot be directed solely towards those who are admirable and virtuous. It has to soften our judgements in relation to people who are at points undeniably maddening and plainly wrong.

A way to conceive of love is as a willingness to look beyond the obvious damning grounds for bad behaviour in search of certain deeper, more forgivable reasons why someone messed up. We see this most clearly in the way that a parent loves a child. When a 3-year-old throws a tantrum and pushes their dinner plate on the floor, scattering pasta everywhere, a parent knows not to slap their offspring and declare them 'evil'. The parent will search for reasons why their child acted as they did. Perhaps they have sore gums. Maybe they are extremely tired. Perhaps their rivalrous feelings towards a sibling have reached a pitch. The parent searches for something other than sheer 'badness' to explain a departure from good sense and decorum.

A little of this curiosity and empathy should, with caveats and boundaries, enter our adult relationships as well. Here, too, there will be plenty of occasions when we cannot easily imagine why our partner acted as they did: their moodiness seems to have no rationale. There can be no blameless explanation for the way they spoke to our friend. Nothing seems capable of excusing their persistent lateness ...

But though outrage may feel liberating, it is no friend of love. In order to stand any chance of working, a relationship has to involve – on both sides – a continuous attempt to drill beneath difficult words and actions in search of their more complicated and occasionally touching origins. Perhaps our partner is feeling sexually insecure; maybe they are unduly threatened by a friend's financial success because they were never allowed to believe that they could matter in themselves. It's possible that persistent lateness is a protest against a bullying, coercive, time-obsessed parent ... Someone may often be a pain and yet still be worthy of a lot of thought and kindness.

Why true tenderness targets the undeserving

At the core of the tender person's outlook is a simple-sounding but love-sustaining move: they treat the other as no less fragile, flawed and sensitive than they remember themselves to be – only around slightly different things. Tenderness taps modestly and perceptively into self-knowledge.

When love is tender, two partners can together develop an impetus for change: the most easily bruised parts of who they are can dare to be exposed because they know that the other's touch will be gentle. The things we despaired that no one could understand about us become, at last, possible to admit to. The strange, sweet aspects of our complicated, troubled minds open up to being explored and accepted in all their lonely oddity and shame.

(iv) A therapeutic attitude

To state it boldly – and to risk sounding somewhat strange – all good lovers are in a way good psychotherapists; that is, the success of modern romantic relationships critically depends on the degree to which both partners can, at crucial moments, adopt a therapeutic attitude towards the other's compulsions, blind spots, rages and eccentricities.

This sounds odd to say because we usually see therapy as something only a professional can do in a consulting room after years of training, rather than as anything that we and a partner might be able to offer one another in the kitchen, the bedroom or over a cocktail in a small but rather elegant bar.

Yet if we drill down into the true nature of psychotherapy, our perspective changes. At base, the discipline relies on a theory about how emotional life works. Powerful emotions – therapy says – are triggered in the present by traumas and difficulties that began in a distant and usually largely forgotten past.

The essence of psychotherapy lies in a willingness to get systematically interested in why we constantly respond in the bizarre and uncalled-for ways we exhibit. It asks by what sequence of formative experiences an otherwise perfectly decent and intelligent person could be led to sob on the floor or threaten to jump out of the window after being asked to tidy a drawer or rewrite a paragraph. It's less disturbed by a tantrum, a sulk or a cold withdrawal than it is curious about where such over- or under-reactions might be coming from.

For therapy, there is always a good – and often moving – story about why someone ends up shouting 'Fuck off you bastard!' at the person they most love or gets icily dismissive when another is pleading for warmth. Perhaps far back, in the old house decades ago, there were genuine, urgent emotional terrors that had to be countered by aggression or evaded by massive psychological withdrawal. While the body has grown, the deep patterns of the mind have stayed the same, so that one now reacts not to what is presently happening but to an old threat that has been unknowingly re-evoked. The brutish words or cold facade are – when the logic of the mind is properly disentangled – directed not at a partner but at a carer, parent or rival in a now hazy, convoluted backstory.

In the consulting room, disturbed feelings can gradually be repatriated so that we no longer unleash them, haphazardly, on whomever happens to be most prominent in our lives. We grow appropriately therapeutic when we can be genuinely interested in the long history that might be standing behind the least alluring and at times appalling emotional conduct of which we and our partners are capable. As therapeutically minded lovers, we no longer always ask why *they* are being so horrible to *us* – we try to work out what *other people* might long ago have done to and around *them*.

We realise that we've come along late in the history of others' souls; they are fighting emotional battles that commenced many years before they could have suspected our existence. They dug themselves into defensive positions or honed their offensive tactics – to which we are now exposed – by the time they were mastering the eight times table. It isn't their fault. They didn't ask to have the childhood they did; they coped as best they could and we, now, are simply the haphazard targets for their largely unconscious – albeit often genuinely off-putting – strategies of defence.

Along the way, psychotherapy teaches us that direct confrontation is seldom a good idea. A therapist might know, pretty much from day one, what a client is suffering from. They might have a solid thesis that the client is mentally scrambled because their mother's abundant love carried with it a secret command that they must never acknowledge any sexual feelings. Or that they are paranoid because of their father's displays of violence and cruelty. But what counts isn't that the therapist has developed an accurate diagnosis, but rather that the patient is allowed to recognise it for themselves, by a process of carefully designed prompts, in a way that they can absorb without fear, in their own time. That is why therapists tend to proceed via gentle questions – 'I wonder how it felt when Mum went away?' – instead of blanket assertions: 'Let me tell you why you are so messed up.'

In relationships, too, therapeutic kindness should mean avoiding direct lectures on the issues we sense in our partners. We try (on a good day) not to say: 'I've seen through you. I know what's wrong with you and why you are running away from me as you are.' We strive instead to nudge the other towards greater self-knowledge at a pace they can benefit from. There are no prizes for trying to initiate others into varieties of self-awareness they have no strength for.

Furthermore, in relationships that work well, the burden of analytic interpretation never falls only on one person; we're both prepared to see each other through an even-tempered therapeutic lens. We can mutually promise: 'I'll be less frightened of what's disturbed yet disguised in you, if you can begin to imagine doing the same for me and my foibles.'

Everyone – in the close-up, prolonged inspection entailed by all relationships – is sure to reveal themselves as being substantially disturbed. Which is why we so want and need to be with someone who grasps, with reference to the complexities of our early emotional lives, the essential normality of our oddities. They might win our hearts by saying, on an early date: 'I'll tell you about how mad I am and where it all began, if you'll tell me how crazy you are and how Mum and Dad messed you up.' We'll thereby be deploying the possibilities of a therapeutically minded perspective to help secure the long-term, sympathetic love we are looking for.

(v) Enthusiasm

When relationships start, our enthusiasm for our partners tends to be at a high pitch. We think of them constantly, we want only to spend more time in their company, we delight in their many skills and accomplishments: we can't quite get over how they know how to glide on a dance floor, prepare such tasty soups, read interesting novels, sweet-talk our hard-to-please mother or calmly perform a life-saving operation on an ailing horse or poodle.

But this early phase of powerful admiration and longing rarely lasts. A few years in, our partner may still be a stylish dancer, a good cook, a knowledgeable thinker, a fixed favourite of our mother or a superlative vet – and yet we now find it hard to feel or express too much wonderment. A sullenness has taken hold of us that does not lift. There is, somewhere deep inside us, a gigantic, stubborn 'but'.

The corrosion of romantic enthusiasm is one of the grand, intimate, tragic and rarely told stories of love. It seems to happen almost without our noticing; we gradually slip into a position of no longer being able to admire very much. With time, we may feel loyal to the union we've built; we may harbour a deep friendship towards our partner; we'd give them a kidney – but we can't relish in and celebrate their merits as we once did.

The world often explains this cooling as a sheer and inevitable result of exposure. It is, they say, typical that we neglect what is always around. But the true reasons seem more comp-licated, more psychologically rich and, in their own way, a lot more hopeful.

If we stop admiring, it is not because we are ever really bored or because it is 'normal' to take someone for granted; it is chiefly only because we are, at some level, furious. Anger creeps into love and destroys admiration. We cease to delight because we unknowingly grow entangled in various forms of unprocessed annoyance. We can't cheer them on because, somewhere deep inside, we are inhibited by trace memories of certain let-downs, large and small, of which they have been guilty without having been informed of it, and which they haven't been able to correct. Perhaps they caused us immense difficulties around a work crisis and never apologised. Maybe they flirted with a friend of ours and left us feeling tricked and unsure. They may have booked a holiday without asking us and then insisted that they'd done nothing wrong.

Every infraction was not, on its own, necessarily always particularly serious, but taken cumulatively, a succession of minor disappointments can acquire a terrible capacity to dampen and ultimately destroy ardour. Yet it is not the simple fact of being let down that counts very much – the true problem is created when there hasn't been an opportunity to process our disappointment. Irritation is only toxic when it hasn't been extensively and thoughtfully aired.

Perhaps we tried to explain what was wrong but we got nowhere. The partner lost their temper and we gave up. Or, more subtly, we might not have felt entitled to make a fuss over so-called 'small things' and therefore stayed silent even though, in our depths, the small things mattered immensely to us. With great unfairness to our partner, we may have forgotten to admit to our own sensitivities even as we developed a steady burden of resentment against their unknowing offences.

What follows from such buried anger is something that can be mistaken for disinterest but is in substance very different. We no longer want to celebrate their birthday; we withhold sexual attention; we don't look up when they walk into a room. This could seem like the normal impact of time and proximity, but it is no such thing. It is evidence of cold fury. We do our anger an honour, and can start to dismantle its deleterious effects, when we recognise the full impact of unexamined frustration on our emotions. We never simply go off people; we only ever get very angry with them. And then forget we are so.

To refind our instinctive enthusiasm for our partner, we need to accurately locate our suppressed distress. We have to allow ourselves to be legitimately upset about certain things that have saddened us and properly raise them – for as long as we need to – in a way that lets us feel acknowledged and valued. Because anger inflicts an ever-increasing toll the longer it is left unaddressed, a good couple should allow for regular occasions when each person can – without encountering opposition – ask the other to listen to incidents, large or small, in which they felt let down of late. There might be an evening a week left free for this form of 'processing'. The mission should be bluntly known to both parties: *an opportunity to pick up on areas in which we feel let down* – not, one should add, in the name of killing love, but in the name of ensuring its ongoing buoyancy. It goes without saying that we might not immediately see why a given thing should matter so much to our partner, but that wouldn't be the point. The objective of the exercise would never be to listen to complaints that seemed utterly relatable to us, it would be to let the partner know that we cared because these were problems in their minds.

To ensure that our desire never suffers, this kind of hygienic ritual might be placed at the centre of every relationship. If couples too often ignore the requirement, it is because they operate under an unfair burden of bravery: they are far more susceptible than they let themselves think. They assume that it cannot be sane to get 'upset' so often, to experience so much hurt, to be so easily ruffled. They can't summon the courage to make a complaint about things that they don't even admit to themselves have caused a sting – and so they stay silent until it is no longer possible for them to feel.

Wiser couples know that nothing should ever be too small to cover at length – for what is ultimately at stake in a marathon conversation about a single word or a miniscule event in the hallway can be the fate of the entire relationship. These lovers are in this sense like wise parents who, when a child is sorrowful, are patient enough to enter into the imaginative realm of the child and take the time to find out just how upsetting it was that the felt-tip pen smudged the top of the drawing of the daffodil, or that their teddy bear 'Nounou' didn't get to eat 'lunch' at nursery. It might, in a similar spirit, not be silly at all to devote three and a quarter hours to understanding why a partner got silently immensely upset by the way we said the word 'ready' to them at breakfast the day before, or how it felt to them when we were a touch slow at laughing along with a mildly unfunny story they shared about a train and a suitcase at dinner with our aunt. The gratitude that will flow from such an effort to understand them will be amply repaid the next time we feel abandoned because they forgot to put the lid back on the olives or omitted to add a second 'x' at the end of an email.

To complain in love is a noble and honourable skill very far removed from the category of whininess with which it is sometimes confused. The irony of well-targeted and quickly raised complaints is that their function is entirely positive. Honesty is a love-preserving mechanism that keeps alive all that is impressive and delightful about our partner in our eyes. By regularly voicing our small sorrows and minor irritations, we are scraping the barnacles off the keel of our relationship and thereby ensuring that we will sail on with continued joy and admiration into an authentic and unresentful future.

2.

Preparations for Love

One of the alluring but terrible deceptions our societies try to sell us is that the predominant challenge of love lies in finding 'the right person'. Once we have – after a long chase and many auditions – discovered this elusive character, we will apparently then be able to relax our efforts and settle into long-term contentment.

On the back of this idea, we have collectively built an industrial-scale economy focused on ways of bringing people together. This is billed as 'finding love', but really all it provides us with is the opportunity to meet someone – while the vastly more complex and challenging task of knowing how to love them continues to go unaddressed.

Yet the reality is that, however many enticing people we are connected up with, we will have little chance of building a successful relationship with them unless we have first mastered the psychological virtues required to sustain affection. There is no point in 'dating' until we have understood the nature of loving.

Even before anyone enters our lives, there is therefore value in developing our capacity to love – and in honing our understanding of the five skills essential to its flourishing.

A questionnaire to develop the five skills of love

(i) *Nondefensiveness*

- What criticisms have stung you in the past?
- Might there have been any truth in them, even if they were meanly expressed?
- How did you respond? How, ideally, might you have responded?
- Ask a trusted and kind friend to say one critical thing about you; note your emotions (the possible spasms of hurt, outrage or fear). Dare to ask for further information – and to trust that your friend does not suddenly, mysteriously, 'hate' you.
- Are you in theory able to imagine being loved and criticised at the same time?

(ii) *Vulnerability*

- What might you be embarrassed to admit to a partner (around money, sex, politics, career mishaps, personal habits, tastes, regrets)? Be as frank as possible, in the deep privacy of your mind. Then, with care and courage, choose a friend to make an initial confession to. And then another.

- One day, tell someone that you miss them terribly.
- Note what is most 'babyish' in you and reframe your longings and fragilities in a less shame-filled direction.
- In what ways might everyone be, for better and for worse, childish?

(iii) *Tenderness*

- Think of something a person might do that would seriously offend you (they tell a blatant lie, they freeload, they do something sexually unusual). What would be the kindest explanation for their conduct?
- When have you done something that might offend a virtuous onlooker? Try to account for, and then look imaginatively upon, your own behaviour.
- Employ similar generosity towards another person who has failed or done something you disapprove of.
- Reflect on what twists of fate might, in a slightly different version of your life, have meant that you did something you abhor.

- Read the newspaper and pick out two 'villains' who have done unfortunate things. Try to imagine them as newborns. How would you consider their fate with tenderness?

(iv) A therapeutic attitude

- What was emotionally tricky in your own childhood – even if everyone meant substantially well?
- What 'scars' has the past left on your adult personality?
- What about you is unbalanced or extreme?
- How have your assumptions about other people 'in general' been unfairly coloured by experiences with specific people in your early years?
- What are the main ways in which you defend yourself against unbearable truths about who you are?

(v) Enthusiasm

- Reflect on a friendship that has, over the years, gone cold. Analyse what 'small' hurts might lie beneath your corroded affection. Dare to tell a friend about what in their behaviour upset you.
- How good are you at pointing out irritations and wounds to others? How well can you clear the air so that the channels of admiration are unblocked?

- Imagine gently explaining to someone that they have – inadvertently – made you feel sad or angry. How does this make you feel?

★★★

These are painfully complicated questions and prompts. They probe at things we rarely recognise or acknowledge in ourselves. We may need to revisit these exercises at intervals to settle and refine our answers. But they are showing us two big things. Firstly, that we might not automatically be ready to make a relationship succeed. Secondly, that the qualities that help relationships work are open to education and development. We can (like someone taking driving lessons) improve on what we need to know. Nurturing love is the business of a lifetime; the idea that we may not be entirely ready for the task ahead is not an insult. It's a sane and hopeful recognition of the scale and importance of the enterprise upon which we seek to embark.

3.

Learning to Love Oneself

No animal can hate itself, perhaps, except – of course – a human being. It's one of the strangest and most regrettable flaws in our condition. We may hardly even have noticed our settled tendency towards self-disgust, which probably shows up as a persistent substratum of sadness or a compulsion to ruminate on our errors and to anticipate disaster. As victims of self-hatred, we cannot forgive ourselves for the many sickening and abhorrent things we've done; we are never far from remembering how much we've messed up our lives, how we've let others down and the ways in which we're excessively weak, deceptive or ugly.

This settled tendency towards self-hatred is not only destructive of our spirit, it also constantly undermines our efforts to establish workable relationships, for it is logically impossible to allow anyone else to love us while we remain obsessed by the thought of our own loathsome natures. Why let another think better of us than we think of ourselves? If anyone did step forward and try to be kind to us, we would have to despise them with the intensity owed to all false flatterers.

It therefore turns out that one of the central requirements of a good relationship is – surprisingly – a degree of affection for our own natures, built up over the years, largely in childhood. We need a legacy of feeling very deserving of love in order not to respond obtusely and erratically to the affections granted to us by adult partners. Without a decent amount of self-love, the love of another person will always be prone to feeling sickening and misguided, and we will self-destructively – though unconsciously – set out to repel or disappoint it. It will simply be more normal and more bearable to be rejected.

We can investigate our core attitude towards ourselves via certain targeted questions:

Exercise

How ready would you be to agree – in your most private moments – with the following statements?

- I don't like how I look.
- I have not lived up to my potential.
- I am not proud of my career.
- I am not as creative and successful as I should be.
- I am sexually insufficient.
- I have let everyone down.
- No one would want me.
- No one impressive could approve of me.
- I am not a good person.
- I should not exist.

The more statements we agree with from this list, the closer we are to the self-hating end of the spectrum. We should not continue to imagine that love could be easy, even if the most accomplished person were to enter our lives – indeed, especially if they were to make the error of doing so. Our underlying disgust at our own being would only create a harrowing conflict. We would recognise that another was offering us their deep affection, but in the secret folds of our souls, we could only be certain of a mistake or delusion. We would have to reject, recoil, not follow up, push away and in a thousand small and large moves ensure that a lover would eventually have to align their view of us with our view of ourselves.

To begin to counterbalance the hatred, we have to learn to extend compassion to ourselves for our self-lacerating impulses, and remember that how we feel about ourselves is – we can be certain – a bitter legacy of how other people, at a formative age, viewed and treated us.

Exercise

How did we arrive at the tragic conviction that no one could know us and love us at the same time?

Complete the sentences:

- *My mother made me feel I was ...*
- *My father made me feel I was ...*
- *From my early years, I learnt I was essentially ...*
- *My past taught me that my body was ...*
- *The younger me believed that I deserved ...*

The adult process of recovery involves grasping that we have indeed absorbed unduly harsh ideas about who we are, but that it is entirely in our power to begin to counteract them by imagining how a better caregiver might have supported us in the past – and how a kind lover might help us in the future. An ideal, compassionate figure would have known at the start never to equate lovability with perfection; they could have cared for us despite our coming last in the race, our missteps and our confusions.

Exercise

We need to build compassion for ourselves. Try answering these questions:

- How should we treat ourselves?
- If we saw a friend treating themselves as we treat ourselves, what would we advise?
- Looking forward, how might we dare to respond if someone one day decided we were really rather lovely?
- Could we forgive someone who did not have contempt for us?
- How might we overcome the nauseous feeling of realising that we were admired and adored?

The phrase 'self-love' misleads us when we imagine that searching for it would mean striving to acquire a conceited, pompous view of ourselves. True release from self-loathing tends to be a great deal more modest: we are only after a sane, fair and more accurate perspective on our ordinary earthly nature. We can, with kindness and good humour, accept that being silly is entirely normal; wasting opportunities is universal; average sexuality is to be expected. Self-love shouldn't be predicated on the competitive idea that we must pull off extraordinary feats of courage or intelligence. True love is only ever the compassion of the fallen for the fallen; it's the search by one radically imperfect being to express their tenderness at the sight of the struggles and pains of another. We should – henceforth – allow ourselves enough self-love to be able to endure a little kindness.

4.

Knowing What to Overlook

Many people, after they've been in a couple for some time, will privately admit that they are – in many ways – frustrated and disappointed by the person they've chosen to share their lives with.

If pressed for details, they will have no difficulty coming up with a list. Their partner, they might complain:

- is too loyal to their irritating family
- doesn't share their views on the layout of the living room
- never wants to go on camping holidays
- plays tennis every Wednesday evening, no matter what
- doesn't like Moroccan food
- doesn't share their enthusiasm for 19th-century Russian novels
- has a friend who laughs for no apparent reason
- likes doing jigsaws
- drinks coffee from a big mug with '1984' inscribed on the side

- has a habit of adding 'actually' to every second sentence, when it's actually redundant

As the list gets longer, they sigh; they still love their partner and long to be happy together, it's just that it seems impossibly complicated to make this relationship work.

What's driving the frustration isn't that they have sadly fallen for an idiot as a mate; it's rather that we have all inherited needlessly complicated ideas of what relationships might be for. We are told that love is meant to involve the almost total merging of two lives: we expect that a loving couple must live in the same house, eat the same meals together every night, share the same bed, go to sleep and get up at the same time, only ever have sex with (or even sexual thoughts about) each other, regularly see each other's families, have all their friends in common – and pretty much think the same thoughts on every topic at every moment.

It's a beautiful vision, but a hellish one too, for it places an impossibly punitive burden of expectation on another human. We feel the partner must be right for us in every way, and if they're not, that they must be prodded and cajoled into reforming.

But there's another perspective from which to evaluate our needs: relationships don't have to be so complicated and ambitious if we keep in view what in the end actually makes them fulfilling. If we boil matters down, there are – as we have seen – only five essential things we want from one another:

i.   A mutual, nondefensive readiness to admit to imperfections.
ii. A willingness to let ourselves be vulnerable.
iii. A generous, compassionate response to our flaws and errors.
iv. A therapeutic reaction to what is 'mad' inside both of us.
v.   A sufficient lack of anger to keep admiration alive.

When these big, underlying themes are in place, it's not that the other irritants or points of difference will magically disappear. They'll still be there, but our perspective on them will alter.

Everyone is, at some level, a wounded animal, a broken creature. The encounter between two such beings can only ever be fractious at points. A degree of pessimism underwrites hope. We'll never find someone who agrees with us at all moments, but we may discover a partner who can see – and soothe – our existential loneliness, be tender towards our sadness and sympathetic to our less edifying aspects. We can accommodate almost any number of divergences in taste, background and intellect if the central emotional attitudes are secure.

By limiting what we expect a relationship to be about, we overcome the tyranny and bad temper that bedevils too many initially hopeful unions. A bond between two people can be deep and important precisely because it is not accompanied by boundless expectation, nor played out across all practical details of existence. By simplifying – and clarifying – what a relationship is for, we release ourselves from overly complicated fantasies – and can focus instead on our urgent underlying need for sympathy, generosity, tenderness, honesty and warmth.

5.

Knowing When to Be Demanding

Seducers on a search for love tend to oscillate between a fear of being too demanding and an equally intense horror of compromising too readily. What, then, should we be firm in wanting? And what, correspondingly, can we afford to let go of?

Being demanding – drawing attention to a problem and not giving up until it is addressed and even, if need be, making a scene – cannot always be unwarranted. It must at points be as unwise to back down as it is, at others, to keep pushing ahead. There are lives doomed because, at a key moment, someone bit their tongue and stayed quiet when they should have had the bravery of their instincts. On an aeroplane, for instance, it may be uncalled for to make a fuss when the sandwiches run out, but if the person next to us is quietly loading a handgun, a grave response is evidently in order. We should beware of invariably privileging an uncomplaining, temperate life.

What then, in relationships, should we be demanding about? What are the deep, potentially fatal threats to mutual existence that we must strive never to compromise over? The things we have to make an intelligent fuss about concern our core emotional requirements. Although these present in infinitely varied individual versions, they broadly give rise to our five fundamental demands. Our requests to our lovers might sound like this:

1. I need you to accept (more often and more readily) the possibility that you might be at fault, without this feeling like the end of the world to you. You have to allow that I can have a legitimate criticism and still love you. I need you to be less defensive.

2. I need you to own up to what you are embarrassed or awkward about in yourself. I need you to know how to access the younger parts of yourself without terror. I need you to be able to be vulnerable around me.

3. I need you to respond warmly, gently and compassion-ately to the fragile parts of who I am, and to listen to and understand my sorrows. We need a union of mutual tenderness.

4. I need you to have a complex, nuanced picture of me, to understand the emotional burdens I'm carrying – even though I wish I weren't – from the past. You have

to see me with something like the generosity associated with therapy.

5.   I need you regularly to air your disappointments and irritations with me – and for me to do the same with you – so that the currents of affection between us can remain warm and our capacity for admiration intense.

When we're not getting what we need around these foundational themes, we have every right to notice, escalate and explain our requirements. If the other tries to brush us off, we would be wise to keep pushing. If they never engage, we should accept that we are on a path to untenable difficulties.

There are several entirely understandable – but not irremovable – obstacles in the way of becoming constructively demanding about our needs. One is that we often fail to swim sufficiently far upstream to reach the problems we are actually trying to target. We don't carefully search out the underlying issue that is powering our disappointment and stick instead to its surface triggers. We might, for example, get immensely worked up that a partner arrives for lunch at a restaurant nine minutes late, and we might then berate them at length for their tardiness. However, what we could in essence be trying to complain about – if only we could realise it – is something more complicated and

59

prior to the issue in our sights: a feeling that our new lover is not emotionally trustworthy, that despite their charm they are somehow flighty and unresolved. Yet this real explanation for our mood and our fear might elude us. We might stick to levelling our complaint at a practical issue as opposed to picking up on the psychological trait that animates it. We risk coming across as unfairly and oddly worried about timekeeping, tidiness or spelling when, in reality, our worries are motivated by a more poignant, global and legitimate fear about the other's emotional capacities.

We also stumble when an insecurity about our right to make a demand renders us alternately too quiet and then overly angry. We say nothing for too long and then give way to a pent-up expression of frustration and bitterness that, in its wild intensity, is guaranteed not to win us the careful attention of the partner that we were seeking. A patient explanation of why we need them to understand a piece of our past and grow less guarded in their description of their family can disappear because of a snap decision to call them a cock and slam the door. We may want to say certain things very badly – and yet we have to learn how to explain them to our partner as if we didn't especially.

Our childhoods may not have helped us in this regard. They may have chiefly introduced us to outbursts, entitled indignation, brutal put-downs and wild accusations. We may seldom have seen a mature version of being demanding in action: the judged lead-up, the calm but clear tone, the broad atmosphere of appreciation, the assumption that misunderstandings can – with time and goodwill – be resolved and the sure faith that the other is not a monster if they have let us down. We may have failed to pick up on the distinction between assertion and aggression – the latter motivated by a desire to hurt the partner, the former by a hope of educating them.

All this being said, we shouldn't neglect the risks associated with being naively hopeful too early on that we must have landed on the right candidate. We may be so frightened that we have not met the one that we neglect to explore whether or not we have actually done so. We have to be substantially at peace with the idea of being single for many years in order to ride out the ups and downs of dating life. The horror of needing to restart the search can bend our minds unwisely towards the wrong kind of compromise and acceptance. We should be wary of dropping our demands too lightly: the consequences of an unsuitable candidate make themselves felt over long and very lonely years. The character trait that began as a minor source of irritation will, compounded over time, acquire the power to wreck our lives – like a proverbial pebble in a shoe that, when we walk with it around the house merely scratches our heel, but over the course of a ten-mile marathon can shred our foot to a pulp.

We certainly don't need anyone to be perfect, but we should learn to run away very early from those who cannot listen to feedback, who cannot be tender, who have no sure grasp of their or our psychological histories and who have no interest in the work of rupture and repair. To insist on these points isn't to be fussy; it's to be rightfully aware of the terrifying consequences of emotional misalignment.

6.

Confidence in One's Weirdness

One of the secret obstacles to forming a good relationship lies in the strength of our longing to appear normal.

This is particularly evident in the early days of love, when – over dinner – we explain what we are like and, without any obvious wish to deceive, present ourselves as substantially normal, free of unusual or burdensome habits, without distinctive and powerful appetites – simply a reliable, kind, healthy, optimistic and wholly unalarming Everyman or -woman.

The impulse to clean up our natures is easy to understand. We are, after all, attempting to ensure that our isolation will come to an end. But the costs of our airbrushing tend, over time, to be immensely high. In the course of moulding ourselves into a shape we think will appeal, we sacrifice multiple aspects of our reality that will not ultimately let themselves be easily forgotten and that will complain at our attempts to repress them by unleashing symptoms, twitches and compensatory cravings. We cannot faithfully ignore the self that wakes up a little after 4 a.m. every morning in a panic, that eats too much to escape a sense of sorrow, that is interested in certain byways of sex, that is terrified of entering a room of strangers, that is uncommonly alarmed by features of their career and that is intermittently sure of dying broke, disgraced and alone.

The paradox of love is that we both desperately long to be known and fear that we will be rejected if we ever are so. The way out of our furtiveness is to come to a more reasonable view of what is, despite appearances, likely to be happening in other people's minds as well. We cannot – considered logically – have been formed in the utterly unique ways we fear on a planet of nearly 8 billion souls. Much that we consider to be wholly abnormal in ourselves must have counterparts in others, even those who insist on presenting themselves as respectable and unblemished. The terrors, the appetites, the weaknesses, the idiocies – these cannot be our burdens alone, and we can dare to believe that they must exist somewhere within the mind of the ostensibly reasonable person seated opposite us at an early dinner.

With a background confidence in the universality of strangeness, we should take steps to share some of the following ideas early on in our unions, so as not to have to collide into them awkwardly down the line. We should tell our companions that:

We are scared

As everyone is, about pretty much everything. Life is an alarming business for well-founded reasons. A blood clot could mean that we are dead by nightfall; an economic downturn could wipe out every one of our advantages; a rumour could destroy our name.

We are emotionally scarred

None of us came through childhood unharmed. We have all – in response to the odd characters we encountered there – taken on peculiar defences and modes of being that render us overly aggressive or under-confident, chaotic or rigid, preoccupied or thoughtless. A 'normal' person has yet to be born.

We are not as grown up as we seem

The child in us lives on and is neither necessarily charming nor benevolent. They have tantrums; they sulk rather than explain; they want to be rescued but may bite those who try to do so. Very often, they simply feel sorry for themselves. It's touching – almost.

We are sexually unlike what we are 'meant' to be

Every era bequeaths its participants with a script about what normal sexuality looks like and demands. Every era thereby compels its members to lie or feel intensely ashamed about a lot of who they are. We are no exception. We know what – despite the apparently 'liberated' atmosphere we breathe – we have never dared to tell anyone. The risk of being thought a sinner or a pervert hounds us every bit as much as it would one of our medieval ancestors cowering guiltily from the prohibitions of a severe priest or imam.

Our dinner companions might be tempted to run, but they should – in response to our candour – be uncommonly interested in staying, given the extent to which relationships are reinforced by mutual authenticity.

In the deeper intimacy of coupledom, our oddities are either going to leak out (to potentially disastrous effect), or the burden of lying about who we are will eventually suffocate our capacity to feel. It is of course painful to list the sorts of things that make us afraid of being too odd to be loved, but there is so much strangeness all around, our quirks are likely to be the rule rather than the exception. A brief survey of curious cases would include a 32-year-old who sucks their thumb; an airline pilot who wants to be breastfed; a professional soccer player who writes poetry; an ambitious male politician who wears dresses; an apparently confident brain surgeon who is terrified of going into shops; someone successful who, with half their mind, is sure they are about to fail; or a rather nice-looking person who has to vomit every time they catch their reflection in the mirror.

We know that 'oddness' is systematically under-reported on the basis of one central fact: to date, we have seldom told anyone the truth about who we are. We believe others are normal and, to return the punishment, we force them to think we might be normal as well. We will finally allow ourselves to be properly warmed by one another's love when we can grow bold enough to escape the prison of our needlessly respectable self-presentations.

Exercise

1. Collect your courage and write down (in invisible ink if need be) something you feel inwardly awkward about in yourself, something you can't bring yourself to confess to a potential partner – even though it isn't, in fact, any kind of betrayal. It's embarrassing, but for no good reason.

2. Write down – at as great a length as possible and going into maximum detail – the actual story of how this 'oddity' emerged in your life.

3. Polish your oddity, organise it, focus on the key points. Practise saying it. Rehearse it in front of the mirror. Be completely solid in knowing that it deserves to be sympathetically grasped by someone you are interested in.

4. Tell them. Early on.

7.

A Test for Rightness

Every early date is – beneath the surface – a test for rightness. It constitutes a covert attempt to determine – alongside the drinks and the pasta, the order of garlic bread and the chat about the traffic – whether someone can be right for us over a lifetime. There is nothing either casual or lighthearted about the procedure.

The problem lies in knowing what the criteria for assessment should be. Our societies are profoundly unhelpful on this score. They lead us to think about looks, sexual appeal, education levels, respectability, status and career prospects.

These are understandable factors, but they leave aside the active ingredients that underpin the long-term viability of a relationship. In place of the socially sanctioned criteria, we might think of a list of questions for prospective lovers based on a range of alternative, psychologically focused elements. We might, over the early encounters, wonder about some of the following:

Questions to raise about a prospective partner

- Can this person apologise for their problematic sides?
- Do they have a keen sense of their flaws?
- Can they accept criticism?
- Are they keen to improve themselves in a psychological sense? Do they know that progress in emotional maturity is desirable or possible?
- Can they say sorry, warmly and generously?
- Can they tolerate flaws – your flaws?
- Do they have a rich interpretive model of where flaws come from?
- Are they curious about the details of your inner life, especially events before you were 9 years old?
- Are they comfortable revealing to you when they are upset? Can they be brave enough to share their disappointments? Can they ask for repair when you damage things inadvertently?
- Can they laugh at themselves and at you with generosity and sympathy at the obvious chaos and disappointment of being human?
- Can they reveal the intensity of their fears and longings? Are they able to access the younger version of themselves?

- Can they allow you to parent their younger self occasionally?
- Can they parent your younger self occasionally?
- Can you be 'mummy' and 'daddy' to each other, as it were, when needed?
- Are they patient with, and curious about, the madness of the human mind?
- Have they made their peace with imperfection?

What the test reveals is that, to a strange and important extent, we're not looking for someone who is objectively impressive; we're trying to home in on the broken individual who can like us in our own secret complexity and whose admitted strangeness we, in turn, can embrace and be comforted by.

8.

Knowing Our Pasts

Some of the most alarming people we ever risk meeting in the course of any search for love are those who insist that – despite the odds – they had a 'happy childhood', and even more provocatively, that their parents were 'normal'.

Such declarations tend not to be symptoms of health so much as harbingers of shortfalls in self-awareness. The chances of anyone having come through the gauntlet of childhood and adolescence without injury are slight in the extreme; the likelihood of having been parented by exclusively mature individuals is even smaller. The goal is never to aim to be a psychologically uncomplicated person, but simply to know – in as much detail as possible – some of the ways in which we can never be so. The characters to fear aren't ever those who have substantial problems – it is those who can't grasp at any close level of detail what their problems might actually be.

This explains the centrality of the enquiry 'How are you mad?' within the early dating rituals. The question does not mean to persecute or accuse; it is intended to give space for two people to show, in unhurried, nonjudgemental ways, the soundness of their grasp on the wiring of their own psyches.

Exercise

What is it that we might need to know of the developmental challenges in ourselves and another?

Trust

- How able are we to believe that another person might sincerely like us?
- How able are we to believe that someone might seem kind, but still – for their own reasons – be out to hurt us?
- How do our patterns of trust and suspicion fit into events in our pasts?

Communication

- How easily can we tell someone that they have disappointed us?
- How easily can we tell someone that we like them?
- How prone are we to fall into a sulk? Why do we imagine we might do so?

Vulnerability

- How ready are we to show someone else the small, fragile, unimpressive version of ourselves?
- Would we let another adult 'baby' us at points? How does the question feel?
- Can we believe that we could be known and still liked?

Childhood narratives

- What went wrong at the start?
- How annoyed do you feel about being asked about the early years?
- What complications has your mother caused you? And your father?
- How are you damaged?

It sounds improbable and even insulting to persist with the idea that how we can get on in a relationship as adults should be so closely connected to what happened when our bike still had its training wheels. We may balk at having to discount the massive addition of experience in the intervening years – but we would be even more at risk if we didn't.

Exercise

Try answering these questions about your relationship with the parent of the gender you're attracted to:

- How giving and warm were they emotionally?
- What was their relationship to their own sexuality?
- Did they make you feel they could be relied upon?
- How did they express annoyance, or need? How has this influenced you today?

The core trajectory of our questions is to help reveal that – even if it was a long time ago and even if we don't wish to pin blame crudely on anyone – we have internalised a less-than-perfect legacy. We have been left to navigate our adult love lives on the basis of a complex inherited template.

Every childhood is guaranteed to lend us a variety of psychological excesses and deficiencies. Acknowledging a troubled emotional history doesn't automatically make a distortion disappear, but it may radically change our perspective on ourselves – and, in turn, allow a partner to be more sympathetic around our trying behaviours (we can forgive rather a lot, once we have a sound narrative about where a problem originated). We may, after long periods of introspection, still feel the impulse to be controlling about a partner's routines or timekeeping – but once we understand the link between our emotions and, for example, a father's early unreliability or a mother's sadism, we can be newly aware that our suspicion and our questioning aren't any sort of reasonable response to a partner's actual needs.

Sometimes, with a psychological history in mind, we will know how to be kinder to ourselves. Instead of getting worked up that our partner has mispronounced a French word or mentioned (for the third time this evening) that we are spending too much money, we will feel sorry for ourselves for the unhelpful dynamics in our pasts that now make such things feel – at points – unbearable to us. We will weep rather than shout.

The person who sees and admits what went wrong in the past may, in the heat of the moment, still not always be able to prevent themselves from 'acting out', but their chances of subsequent apology rise enormously; they will be able to say sorry from a deep place.

9.

The Temptation to Repeat

One of the most basic rallying cries of lovers at the dawn of the modern age was that people should be allowed to love 'whomever they wanted'. Rather than love being dictated by concerns about prestige, money and lineage, our choice of partner was to be left wholly up to us. Our affections were to flow in whatever direction we pleased. Freedom was to replace tyranny.

This has long sounded like an eminently reasonable idea from which we can expect uncomplicated happiness to follow. But it misses a central quirk in our emotional make-up: that though we may now be technically free to marry anyone, we are – from a psychological perspective – still heavily constrained in whom we can find attractive. Our vows may be free; our desires are not. It may not be our families or our societies that oblige us to make certain choices, but we nevertheless remain as heavily constrained as our forebears.

This is because our desires push us towards candidates who – far more than we realise – are connected up with the figures we once loved in childhood. A bedrock idea of modern psychology is that the way we love as adults is conclusively determined by our patterns of love in our early histories. We love in the way that we once loved; we are attracted to those who echo the characteristics of our primary caregivers. Without knowing this is happening, when we find love, we are also always at some level *refinding* love – which may explain lovers' frequent touching sense that their partner is someone they've known all their lives. In the psychological sense, they have.

This pattern of repetition need not necessarily be a problem, except for one detail: it involves privileging familiarity over happiness. Depending on what occurred in childhood, we may be driven to re-enact cycles of discomfort, loneliness or humiliation, because – for reasons we don't understand – this feels like 'home'. We may pick precisely those candidates best suited to paining us in ways that we were once pained. At the same time, we may be unable to muster any authentic attraction for candidates who we know, at an intellectual level, would be far better for us. We may come away from an encounter with someone kind, sane, patient and self-aware and declare, to our own puzzlement, that we simply couldn't find them 'attractive' – by which we may in essence mean that something deep inside us recognised that they would be incapable of making us suffer in the way we need to suffer in order to feel we are loved. They seemed dangerously at risk of being able to fulfil our needs – and so had to be ruthlessly expunged as a threat to our integrity.

Perhaps the most obvious question we need to ask ourselves, once the compulsion to repeat a pattern is on the table, is what our original templates might have been like. We should ask ourselves:

- What was the quality of your relationship with the parent or caregiver of the gender you are attracted to?
- Did you feel they liked you? Did you like them?
- Name three positive adjectives that you associate with your caregivers.
- Name three negative adjectives that you associate with your caregivers.

If our answers lay any blame at the feet of our caregivers, we should be on alert. The difficulty is that our repetitions are unlikely to be crudely obvious. We may not get together with someone 'like' our parent, but we may still be at great risk of falling for someone who makes us feel like our parent once made us feel. For example, a parent might have been a working-class mechanic who left school at 15, and we might have spent our entire young adult lives running away from the bullying and unhappiness we came to associate with them by hanging out in more aesthetic and educated circles. There we might have found a new partner with a PhD in music and a sophisticated manner – someone who we were certain could ensure a very different and far better life for us. But we are not – on this basis alone – necessarily in the clear in the long term, for what might unite both candidates at a subterranean level is the emotions they generate in us. Here, both the factory worker and the oboe player might be identical: both might activate a feeling that we are unimportant to them; both might leave us with the impression that they have other things on their mind. One person might listen to the songs of Schubert and wear velvet slippers around the house; the other might spend the weekends shouting on the football terraces and dress in jeans – but both might, in terms of their impact, be identical. We might have made extraordinary efforts to escape a parent, only to discover that we have, to our horror, unwittingly refound them in disguise.

Some further questions:

- Might you be proposing to marry your mother or father? Cease to think about surface similarities (clothes, accents, jobs, appearance) and concentrate on one thing only: how they make you feel.

- How did the parent of the gender you are attracted to make you feel about yourself?
- How does your partner make you feel about yourself?

To recognise, or admit more clearly than before, that one has been – perhaps for a long time – trapped within a pattern of repetition can initially be highly dismaying. But a diagnosis does not have to determine our future. The crucial step in dismantling the repetition is to notice it. The more we understand why our desire has traditionally been directed towards certain sorts of candidates, the more we are free to push ourselves to deviate from the score, till the moment, one day many years from now, when we might dare to love someone who resembles no one we have ever yet known intimately – that is, someone deeply kind.

But if our partners continue to resemble a difficult parent, managing the issue well still allows us a chance to resolve one of our most fervent wishes from early childhood: that we might have saved a tricky parent from their own worst sides. We could, with a partner modelled on our archetype, have an opportunity to play things out in a way that we were never able to in our early years. Our parent might have been impatient and loud, and we would have loved to slow them down and discover their potential for tenderness, but we had none of the tools to do so. We could barely speak and mostly cowered in terror. Yet around their successor in adult life, we have another chance to resolve things to our satisfaction. Now, with all the benefits of maturity, we can eloquently talk to the partner about their haste and their irritability; we can spend a whole dinner analysing with them why they started to shout, and explore the link between their ill temper and their own histories. Handled with resolve and perspicacity, their defensiveness may crumble, and they might turn out to be both open and grateful. We could frame things calmly and encourage them to look into themselves in a way that would make a decisive difference. We might even manage to persuade them to go to therapy. We'll thereby be pulling off one of the great feats of mature love: arranging for a different kind of ending.

10.

Mastering Projection

Imagine that we decided to carry out a curious exercise of showing a random group of people a photograph and asking them to guess what might be going on in it. The exercise might feel a little unfamiliar at first but – with some encouragement – we might soon find our respondents loosening their imaginations and coming up with a range of plausible scenarios.

Looking at the photograph overleaf, one person might surmise: 'The woman we see on the right is explaining that someone has betrayed her, probably her husband. She's appalled and hurt, and her friend is listening with sympathy. It's terribly raw for her.' Another might decide: 'The two women are about to form a relationship. The woman on the left is feeling nervous, but her date is putting her at ease by talking about art, which she loves very much.' A third could declare: 'They're in the north of England, it's mid-March and they're discussing socialism.'

Key to the exercise is that the photograph has deliberately been chosen because it is ambiguous – that is, it isn't about any one thing; it has no one meaning. We can't know what it is 'about', and therefore what people say is going on in it is – very usefully – likely to tell us more about who they are, what is on their minds and how their personal histories have played out than anything that might objectively have been going on when the photograph was taken.

Ambiguous images are a favourite of psychologists because of the light they can shed on the unconscious workings of their clients' minds. The elaborations that respondents make when they see such images disclose a range of clues as to their underlying obsessions, hurts and desires. This is helpful because of the way our emotional warps tend to distort our perceptions of reality and so undermine us in the pursuit of our goals. Someone who has had long early experience of being belittled and humiliated by male authority may, in contact with colleagues, potential partners or friends, repeatedly and powerfully imagine that their dignity is about to come under attack and so begin shouting or throwing out random accusations. Another with a history of abandonment may read an acute danger of loss and separation into every relationship they get involved in.

To use the technical term, our histories create in us proclivities to 'project', a process whereby we ascribe to potentially innocent or undefined situations certain stories, motives and conclusions that derive from our pasts. We map our peculiarities onto reality. Our projections can make us act against our best interests in situations that warrant none of our interpretative schemes: perhaps no one is trying to do us down; perhaps no one is seeking to leave us. But, sure that they are and that we understand the disaster at play perfectly, we may flare up, make accusations and otherwise ruin what could have been a perfectly workable situation.

Relationships are – inevitably – filled with projections. Sometimes these run in positive directions: we are sure that someone is about to propose to us; we have a powerful impression that we are wanted and thought of as successful. At other times, the projections are more sombre. We think our partner goes to parties because they want to meet someone else; we think they stay up late because they want to avoid coming to bed with us; we think they brush their teeth very carefully because they are robotically obedient to authority. We interpret what a partner does in the light of what we think their behaviour must mean, rather than what it might actually mean.

An immense amount of conflict in any relationship is driven by this difficult dynamic. One partner assumes they know exactly why the other behaves as they do – why they stay silent, why they hesitate, why they get irritated, why they regularly say certain words – and the partner is left to protest (sometimes angrily, often wearily) at what is being conclusively imagined and asserted.

Our past is, as a rule, liable to be a highly misleading guide to what a partner is actually thinking or intending to do – for our parents or early caregivers are not solidly representative of the humans we meet in adult life. Projections can force our partners into exhaustive efforts to correct phantasms that have arisen around them. No (they hasten to tell us), they are not trying to crush our spirit. No, they have no intention of leaving. No, their exuberance isn't a sign that they are about to lose control and drain the household budget. And no, they are not cold and cruel – simply quiet and a little reserved, in their own distinctive way.

We project so avidly because we have no idea that this is what we are doing. The more we can learn to see our distortions, the less inclined we will be to distort.

One of the ways in which we can hope to catch hold of our projections is by asking ourselves to complete a range of generalised sentences at speed – without thinking too much about how we answer:

- *Whenever I open up to someone, they …*
- *Love is …*
- *Men are …*
- *Women are …*
- *Because of sex …*
- *What tends to happen in relationships is …*
- *If someone finds me attractive, they …*
- *If someone doesn't earn much money …*
- *If someone is clever …*

Our answers will reveal some of our abstract principles; yet relationships are the precise opposite of general. They are about one particular person – a unique individual who does not deserve a narrative formed long ago in contact with, and extrapolated from, someone else.

The opposite of projection is curiosity – the desire to find out what someone is genuinely like. We would as lovers ideally never assume that we can know what is involved in the mind of another – and spend much of our time attempting to find out instead. We would carefully and playfully ask the partner how they felt about fidelity or sexuality or money or being late, without writing the conclusion for them, independently and often, in contradiction to their actual views. We would become humblingly aware of how much we think we know what everything means, and remember that, blessedly and helpfully, we usually don't.

11.

Love and Psychotherapy

Lovers and psychotherapists might, at first glance, seem as if they could have very little to teach one another, but an unexpected way of helping our relationships to flourish can be to study how therapists speak to, and approach, the troubles of their patients. The truths of psychotherapy don't belong only to clinical practice; they have widespread application in the bedroom and especially outside the bathroom door at midnight during heated arguments about ostensibly very little. When relationships get difficult – as they invariably will – therapeutic ideas can give us ways to understand and sympathetically cope with many of the stranger parts of ourselves and our partners.

The following therapeutic ideas can prove to be of particular relevance:

(i) Reflective listening

Life constantly brings us into contact with people we care about who – for a range of reasons, perhaps some of them having to do with us – have grown immensely angry or profoundly distressed.

We would – very much – like to calm them down and relieve them of their symptoms, but our techniques for doing so tend badly to miss their targets. We try to tell them 'not to worry', but they slide into even greater panic. We say that, all told, 'it doesn't really matter', but their irritation heightens. We explain to them in a warm voice that they could afford to calm down, and they pick up a pencil and snap it in two in frustration.

We would at such points be advised to lean on a technique pioneered, and much favoured, by psychotherapy: 'reflective listening'. The thesis behind reflective listening is that an important share of our most serious problems have no solutions in any practical sense. There are simply no 'answers' to losing lots of money, being excluded from a social circle or failing in a job. Of course, there might be a few steps that could be taken – applying for a loan, throwing a party or going on a training course – but these are unlikely to be things either that we have not thought about before or that could, if implemented, shave off more than a fraction of our pain.

What psychotherapy realises is that, in our agony, what we desire more than anything, more than we usually even realise, is companionship: for someone else to know that we are suffering and to feel a measure of our pain more or less as we experience it. We yearn for a sense that another person appreciates the scale of our despair and the magnitude of our sense of injustice – while at the same time being deeply suspicious of, and alert to, anyone who might too hastily be trying to make our distress go away. 'Answers' and 'solutions' – because they seek to remove a problem at speed – may in our panicky moments seem indistinguishable from being asked to shut up and talk about something else.

Having fathomed our longing, psychotherapy makes a key innovation: it proposes a way of behaving around a person who is incensed or sad that can give them a strong feeling that they are being understood. Saying 'I know' or 'Oh yes' won't – therapy knows – be quite enough. What we need to do instead is to *paraphrase* what our ailing companion has said, to build sentences that repeat back to them the essence of the difficulty they have expressed but using different words. This form of precis deftly signals two things: firstly, that we have precisely grasped what they have gone through. And secondly, that we have not merely been passively listening; we haven't dumbly and distractedly echoed their exact language as a recording device would. We've taken the trouble to find a fresh set of words for the same story. Their woes have passed, and been sympathetically filtered, through the distinctive channels of our own minds.

An episode of reflective listening might go like this. We hear them say: 'I hate the bloody lecturers at university so much. They ramble and make no sense. I'm taking on huge debts to be there and I might as well be asleep for all the good it will ever do me.' To which we might respond: 'I'm hearing that your course is proving deeply disappointing. You're finding it hard to understand what's really going on. And the faculty don't seem in any way interested in explaining things properly. You're worrying about how much all this is costing and what contribution, if any, this is going to make to your career goals.'

Or someone might tell us: 'I don't see why you jump to such unfair conclusions about me. Why can't you believe that something just slipped my mind? You're always accusing me ...' To which a reflexive listener might answer: 'I'm sensing that you don't feel trusted. You think I don't have enough faith in your good nature and intentions.'

The genius of reflective listening is that on the basis of paraphrasing alone, we can leave our speaker appeased and becalmed. Without anything having ostensibly changed, the incensed or sad person's levels of fear and irritation ebb. The squall passes; hope makes a return. This teaches us just how much 'solutions' may ultimately be overrated. All that we are chiefly in search of when we are at our lowest point is evidence that we are in company.

(ii) Room for darkness

Whenever people tell us their problems, one of our most common, quasi-automatic – and subtly dispiriting – responses is to try to deny the severity of what they have just said to us.

Someone tells us that they haven't been sleeping very well and we respond – with the best of intentions – that not getting a requisite number of hours 'doesn't really matter'. Another person tells us that they didn't get a promotion and we try to be nice by reminding them that 'they are already doing very well as they are'. Were someone to reveal that they were dying, we might – in extremis – be tempted to say: 'But you can't be ...'

Parents are often to be heard performing this manoeuvre on their upset or angry children:

Child: *I'm feeling sad.*
Parent: *Don't be silly, you're not, it's the holidays.*

Child: *I'm really worried.*
Parent: *Darling, that's ridiculous, there's nothing to be scared of in your bedroom.*

The reason for our cheerful rejoinders lies in our unresolved relationship with our own despair, fear and sadness. We seem so unable to square up to awful things in our lives that we have no option but to try to deny that they might have a place in the lives of others. We become sentimental – that is, addicted to airbrushing away the uncomfortable aspects of reality, out of fear, not deafness.

A more evolved relationship with ourselves – of the kind psychotherapists seek to promote – can assuage the itch to deliver upbeat messages by prompting us to make our peace with sorrow. Someone might say that they are sad, and we could in time learn simply (and more helpfully) to answer: 'I hear you.' Another might insist: 'Everything is awful' and we might look them warmly in the eye and respond: 'Yes, it really can feel like that at times.'

The more we listen to the 'sad' messages our companions send us, the less hard they will have to push them. The more we hear, the quieter they can be. Someone who says they want to burn the country down doesn't want to burn the country down; they want to be heard for their deep frustration that their job or family is causing them. They will only become an arsonist if we continue not to listen – not if we do so amply with empathetic good humour. Feelings get less strong, not stronger, once they've been acknowledged. It is a move of exemplary generosity and maturity to let someone be sad and desperate around us without falling for the cruel temptation to say something cheerful.

(iii) Softening language

Much of our trouble in relationships comes down to the force with which we try to assert certain of our ideas to other people – ideas about who they are, what they've been up to and what they are likely to need in order to be happy. An idea of ours may be entirely correct, but the directness with which we attempt to insert it into another's mind can lead them to recoil and reject it almost as a matter of course, with violence and outrage. The truth, if ever it is to reach others' consciousness, has to travel in the softest, most hesitant layers of doubt.

This explains why we'll so often notice psychotherapists talking to their clients in a way that deftly avoids all powerful assertions or declarations. We won't (or should never) catch them saying: 'You're immature' or 'There's no point complaining.' They are unlikely to utter: 'It's your mother's fault' or 'Leave that no-nothing wastrel!'

They will, instead, typically go in for elaborate circumlocutions to ensure that their ideas feel like being stroked by weightless feathers. They will pepper what they say with markers of graceful and mild intent; they will repeatedly use terms like 'perhaps' and 'maybe', 'somewhat' and 'slightly', 'a bit' and 'a touch'. There will be 'a bit of regret' and 'a touch of sadness'; 'somewhat of a difficulty' and 'maybe a reason to fight back'.

These therapists will at the same time be powerfully alive to the benefits of saying 'I feel' ahead of any analysis of their client's behaviour or attitudes. They know how easily we can be panicked by universal judgements, and how much we prefer it when ideas are framed as though they were only ever the thought of one person, as opposed to a verdict of the whole community or the fruit of the mind of God himself. They hence opt for digestible suggestions over thunderous generalisations: 'I *feel* you're withdrawing somewhat' over 'You're in denial'; '*I feel* you might be a touch angry' over 'You're in a rage.' They know that there are magnitudes of difference between 'You're wasting your time' and 'I *feel* you might no longer be getting the results you need'; between 'Don't always blame other people' and 'I *feel* you might be tempted to hold your friend responsible.'

It is common to have vibrant insights into other people's characters that we would deeply like to share with them. It may strike us, suddenly, as if the whole nature of their problem comes down to their mother. Or as if all they need to do is break free from the baleful influence of their younger sister. The issue is not that such insights are necessarily flawed but that they are too potent – in a way that threatens to engage, in a ruinous way, the other's defence mechanisms. Most of what we don't listen to is far from worthless, it just asks too much of us and therefore has to be expelled from the mind to preserve the emotional status quo. There are truths too true to be heard.

A central way to disarm the danger of suffocating others with reality is therefore to resist the urge to tell them what we suspect is wrong, or up, with them. Whatever the provocation and however late the hour, we must never sink to giving out overly direct diagnoses or grand summaries of their condition. There is strictly no point in saying: 'It all comes down to your father' or 'You're afraid of intimacy.' The novice student of psychology may well be tempted to throw around such fascinating and theoretically highly valid ideas, but if their goal is ever to be listened to, they would be advised to reconsider the way they are opting to share their learnings.

Rather than verdicts, we must – in the name of winning over our audience – give off every sign that we are advancing only musings, tentative, wholly speculative ruminations that have nothing firm, decisive or tenacious about them. We really have no clue; we're just throwing something out and we are – almost certainly – wholly wrong.

It is here that we should have recourse to one of the most emotionally compelling formulations in the psychotherapist's vocabulary: I *wonder*. We must take any brute statement – 'You're trying to seduce someone who doesn't want you' – and carefully recast it with an introductory: 'I *wonder* if you're attempting to seduce someone who ...'. We might start with: 'Stop being so rigid about bedtimes' but end up, far more usefully, with 'I *wonder* if you're not putting a bit too much emphasis on routines.'

Such moves may be apparently small, but their impact can be enormous. That it should be so tells us something very poignant about us. We don't want anyone to be too certain about our situation. Especially about those things that might be decisively true but very hard to take on board. We want the gentlest words to help us come to terms with the most arduous insights.

It is a bathetic but unavoidable reality of human nature that what can separate our absorption of a truth from its angry and incensed rejection may be nothing more or less than a very small, soft, gossamery, yet entirely critical 'maybe'.

Perhaps.

(iv) Therapy knows the truth takes time to accept

To an onlooker, one of the strangest aspects of therapy is the sheer length of time it requires. This is especially puzzling because an experienced therapist can typically diagnose the essentials of a person's troubles in one session. And yet a course of therapy can last two or three years, sometimes five or six, at a rate of one appointment a week.

As therapy sees it, the chief difficulty is not to identify someone's problem; it is to help them see, feel and accept it properly. Were the truth to be baldly laid out before most clients, they would leave at once in a mood of incensed fury – we have only limited strength to hear that, for example, our levels of confidence might be connected up with our father's behaviour towards our sister during the early teenage years, or that our anxiety relates to a trauma that occurred before we were 3. The trick is to cut up a diagnosis into such small portions that it can start to sound like common sense and be benevolently absorbed over a lengthy timescale.

Therapy knows that trust is essential, too, if the truth is to be rendered bearable. We have to like our therapist very much, and have experienced them across a range of topics and developed a comprehensive faith in their personality, in order that – when it comes to truly confronting ideas – we can (on a good day) maintain a belief that they are on our side and that they are not simply putting certain thoughts before us in order to cause us pain and bewilderment.

Likewise, we need a partner to have shown us repeated kindness and forbearance before we'll listen when they tell us important but confronting things that our best friends never dared to raise with us – not because they were any kinder, but because they didn't care enough.

Therapy is a school of patience. It changes our notions of plausible time frames. In a therapeutically minded relationship, we're not going to be outraged that after a few weeks with us and two long conversations, our partner still shirks certain responsibilities, still has a wayward notion of punctuality and still can't shed certain sexual inhibitions. These challenges are conceived of as deeply embedded in emotional dynamics that might – quite reasonably – take years to dislodge themselves. With the example of therapy in mind, we will in our own relationships look for tiny signs of progress rather than rapid, radical change around all those behaviours and thoughts that we so wish could vanish at a stroke.

(v) What is not being said

Therapists famously listen to their clients carefully, but as much as they are listening to what these clients are saying, they are equally attuned to what they are not saying, to emotions that should be due given what is being recounted – for instance, a terrible story about loss or neglect – and yet have somehow drifted out of the story, relegated to the unconscious under the weight of untenable psychic pain. Someone might tell a therapist about their father's sudden arrest and six-month stay in prison and end with a small laugh and the remark, 'It was all quite funny really.' But the therapist won't be laughing back.

Their aim will be to reunite their client with their exiled feelings. So they might pause, at the end of an ostensibly cheery tale about something dreadful, and say: 'That must have been very frightening' or 'It seems so unfair really' – and hope thereby to help the client recover contact with their authenticity and truth.

Likewise, a skilled lover will know that pride and misplaced bravery might frequently lead their partner into diversionary behaviours and stories that mask their actual feelings. After returning from a lunch with their mother, they might turn the bitter relationship they have with her into a succession of humorous anecdotes involving the old lady and the waiter. But a tender lover schooled by therapy might add a small rejoinder: 'It sounds like she still manages to hurt you every time you see her. It can't be easy.' We would then, as the partner, perceive that we had landed on that most special of beings: someone who – like the best sort of therapist and the most enticing of lovers – knows us better than we know ourselves.

(vi) Tolerating ambivalence

One of the ideas about which therapy remains most sanguine is that our feelings are seldom pure. There is rarely a love that is not, at some level, accompanied by a kind of hatred, just as there is rarely a disdain that doesn't have a strand of affection concealed somewhere within it.

Therapy knows that there are few loving mothers who do not, at points, wish their babies dead. And there are few respectful, affectionate children who do not fantasise that their parents might be annihilated, if only for a while. It knows, too, that it's wholly normal to love someone and fantasise about having sex with someone else; or to completely forget why we ever committed to a partner only to recover the thread of our story a few hours later. Therapy is unbothered by the strangeness of our disloyal or entangled feelings. It knows that we are all a good deal stranger than we're allowed to admit and it lets us be as unconventional as is helpful without judging or taking fright.

A lover schooled in therapy can adopt a similar sang-froid. Of course there will be moments of intense hatred and declarations of catastrophe and panic, but this is no reason to think a relationship is doomed – just as a 2-year-old child who bites their mother in a fit of frustration in the kitchen is not to be understood as making any long-term statement about their feelings for their progenitor. With the example of therapy in mind, we'll be less upset by squalls, less frightened of viciousness and better able to hear with wry patience that we are apparently a shitfaced bastard who ruined someone's life – only, ten minutes later, to hear an addendum that we are also someone our partner will love for eternity. Anger and irritation don't destroy love; they are inevitable parts of being genuinely close to and extremely dependent on another human being.

***

A therapeutic attitude taps into a proper recognition of the complexity and contradictions of the mind. It prepares us for the notion that if we are ever to make a good, shared life together with someone, we'll have no option but to confront and accept – and in the end finally love – the infinitely strange and wondrous complexity of a fellow human.

12.

Attachment Theory

It's a remarkable testament to the utility of psychoanalysis that a knowledge of one of its central ideas – attachment theory – has become an indispensable requirement for anyone trying to have a relationship. A piece of intellectual argument first devised in a utilitarian child and adolescent clinic in North London in the 1950s by a modest genius of psychology, John Bowlby, has gone on to provide the explanatory motor for almost every relationship in the world. To be able to say to a partner what one's attachment style is – and to hear theirs in return – and to work out what the consequences of this will be is, quite literally, the central solution to many of the tensions and agonies of love.

Attachment theory suggests that all of us have an attachment 'style' in adult love based on the way we were loved as children. There are three main varieties of attachment – and we should, before we go anywhere near a first date, be sure to have a pretty good grasp of which direction we lean in.

The first and most balanced category is known as *secure attachment*. Here we are able to trust in love and not unduly panic whenever problems occur, as they inevitably do – because we have all across our childhoods known the safe, comforting love of a sane adult who was reliable, steady and full of tolerance and patience. If we are secure in adulthood and someone says something frustrating or puzzling, we don't immediately snap back, throw something at them or withdraw. We get curious, we remain sure of our legitimate need for love and of the likelihood that our partner remains, deep down, kind and good; there is simply some misunderstanding, which we can clear up with humour and goodwill over time (there is no hurry).

The second, far more tragic, characteristic way of bonding to others is known as *anxious attachment*. Here we react like the panicky infants we once were to any sign that our partner is not delivering the utterly secure and intense love we so badly need – in compensation for the turbulent childhood we suffered, in which our needs were not respected and our cravings for love not honoured. We may, as anxious lovers, accuse our partner of being a bad person, shout angrily at them or try to control them into submission. At the slightest sign of a problem, we immediately give up on a sense that our partner might be benevolent and simply respond with fury and destructiveness to our underlying alarm. Again, we have been primed by childhood to expect the very worst – and thereby, in a terrible confirmation of our worst fears, tend actually to bring this about.

The third, equally awful kind of attachment is known as *avoidant attachment*, whereby we respond to a perceived threat in love by going entirely cold, withdrawing and ensuring that we aren't exposed for a second to what we imagine is the catastrophe of loving without being adequately loved back. The irony here, too, is that avoidant people bring about the very problem they are seeking to escape. In response to their coldness and terseness, their emotional chill and distance, the most well-meaning partner may end up responding by doing exactly what the avoidant person fears: going away.

How, then, will knowing attachment theory help? At the most basic level, it will help us to know what to do with puzzling or difficult behaviour in others – but also, as importantly, in ourselves. It will give us a vocabulary in which to own up to our madness and be tolerant towards the madness in others. It should open up a space for humour between a couple, in which their mutual insanities can be reflected upon, forgiven and negotiated around.

If we are faced by someone who is shouting at us and telling us we're a useless, bad person, we might think – if we had just arrived from another planet or were a young person starting out in love – that was a sure sign that someone really didn't like us at all and that we should make an exit fast. But attachment theory urges us to adopt a wiser, very different line. This probably isn't in fact any such sign. It's simply evidence that we're dealing with someone who has real difficulty, because of their childhood, telling us that they love us and yet are hurt. It's too risky and exposed for them to do this and that's why they are calling us a shit, not because they hate us, but because it feels intolerable to re-encounter in adulthood a kind of disappointment that evokes a searing childhood let-down.

Equally, attachment theory warns us what to do if we start to sense a sudden drop in affection in our partner. We might surmise that this was a sign that they have gone off us – and leave accordingly. But we should first do something a little more complicated. We need to ask ourselves: *Might I have inadvertently hurt this person and they are not telling me, because they are the victim of a childhood that has left them badly unable to trust that they can dare to make a successful complaint against someone who has slighted them?* We are dealing with a sort of person who will go cold and silent faster than they will explain and never give their partner a chance to repair the damage out in the open. It's brutal and sad, but a lot less sad than them actually having gone off us. They are cold because they love us, and because that love feels so exposing and risky to them. This kind of person might even – in extremis – slip off and have an affair with someone else – again, not because they hate us, but because we have (probably inadvertently) hurt them, and they never, ever want to be in a position of being hurt without some escape route open to them. Though we think we know what an affair is, there is simply no comparing an affair entered into because of a genuine disinterest in someone with an affair entered into by an avoidant person. One is moving away because they don't love you; the other is moving away because it feels to them that they love you too much in a substantially unrequited way – and the insecurity of doing so has reached a monstrous pitch.

At the same time, attachment theory can give us a clue as to how to behave with our own psyches. If we sense ourselves going cold with a partner, we should think not about how much we dislike them, but about whether or not they have hurt us at some earlier point we can't bear to think about. We're very likely to have gone off them not because they are suddenly awful but because they have damaged our very fragile ability to trust, and we have responded by withdrawing as we learnt to do during our difficult childhoods.

Similarly, if we often find ourselves losing our temper with our partner and throwing all sorts of accusations at them, we should imagine that we aren't merely dictatorial and enraged, we are very scared and that this is why we have become so unpleasant. More importantly, if we can explain this to our partner, they will see that what they have on their hands is not a monster but a very frightened child – which makes all the difference.

Not all relationships deserve to survive, but it's especially tragic that so many of them end because of problems that can so clearly be traced back to difficulties created by unknown attachment issues. We owe it to ourselves, before we leave any relationship, to explore whether what may be driving us out is not a lack of love but a love that feels too frightening, given what our childhoods have taught us about what happens when we need to be loved and soothed. By knowing about attachment theory, we have a chance to break free from the patterns of the past and learn to overcome inevitable but often innocent moments when our partner's love does not seem as solid and unambiguous as we need it to be.

The attachment questionnaire

One of the greatest questionnaires in the history of 20th-century psychology had a modest start in the pages of a local Colorado newspaper, the *Rocky Mountain News*, in July 1985. The work of two University of Denver psychologists, Cindy Hazan and Phillip Shaver, the questionnaire asked readers to identify which of three statements most closely reflected who they were in love with.

To hugely improve our chances of thriving in relationships, we should dare to take the same test:

A.   *I find it relatively easy to get close to others and am comfortable depending on them and having them depend on me. I don't often worry about being abandoned or about someone getting too close to me.*

B.   *I find that others are reluctant to get as close as I would like. I often worry that my partner doesn't really love me or won't want to stay with me. I want to get very close to my partner, and this sometimes scares people away.*

C.   *I am somewhat uncomfortable being close to others; I find it difficult to trust them completely, difficult to allow myself to depend on them. I am nervous when anyone gets too close, and often, others want me to be more intimate than I feel comfortable being.*

Behind the scenes, the options refer to the three main styles of relating to others first identified by John Bowlby, the inventor of attachment theory.

Option A signals a *secure* pattern of attachment, whereby love and trust come easily.

Option B refers to the *anxious* pattern of attachment, where one longs to be intimate with others but is continuously scared of being let-down and often precipitates crises in relationships through counter-productively aggressive behaviour.

Option C is the *avoidant* pattern of attachment, where it feels much easier to avoid the dangers of intimacy through solitary activities and emotional withdrawal.

Questionnaires in newspapers are rarely of much use, but Hazan and Shaver's is the momentous exception. If there is one thing we should do to improve our relationships, it is to know which of the three categories we predominantly belong to – and to deploy this knowledge in love, so as to warn ourselves and others of the traps we might fall into.

We then need a little training because half of us at least are not secure in love; we belong in the camps of either the avoidant or the anxious, and we have – to complicate matters – an above average propensity to fall in love with someone from the other damaged side, thereby aggravating our insecurities and defences in the process.

Here is a brief list of what avoidant and anxious types should keep in mind in their relationships.

If you are an avoidant person with an anxiously attached partner:

- Recognise the extent to which you check out emotionally when things are intense, particularly when there is an offer of closeness.
- Recognise how you will tend to prefer sex and closeness with strangers and how nervous you will be around cuddles and kissing. You probably don't want the light on either.
- Watch how you sabotage long-term intimacy.
- Have compassion for the fact that you are afraid of what you really want.
- Think back to how, in your past, closeness would have been frightening because people let you down, and observe how you adopted a strategy of removal to protect yourself. You are hurt, not bad.

- Remind yourself that the present is different from the past and that you are ruining the present by bringing to it fear-laden dynamics that don't belong there.
- It may feel like your partner is being aggressive and ill-tempered with you for no reason; they are at heart upset and unable to express their needs in any other way. They want you, and that is why they are behaving as they are.
- Look beneath their nagging and their accusations and believe in their underlying goodwill.
- When they attack you, see their longing for love.
- Do that very frightening thing: extend reassurance. And explain, calmly, the appeal of the cave.

If you are an anxious person with an avoidant partner:

- Things are not necessarily as bad as they seem.
- Their quiet might just be quiet, not a lack of love. Their distance isn't meanness, it's their way of maintaining equilibrium.
- You are not 'needy' for wanting more, but your way of dealing with what you legitimately need is aggravating things hugely.
- You are triggering your partner by asking for intimacy too directly and also (probably) with too much anger.

- Realise that you need to tread lightly and be a little distant in requesting closeness.
- The partner isn't mean or freakish, merely damaged – as are you. And that's very normal. A full 40% of the population are in your positions.

Knowing whether we can be classed as secure, avoidant or anxious in love should be a basic fact we grasp about ourselves. The next step is to accept with grace that if we are either avoidant or anxious, we will need considerable emotional schooling to get out of scratchy patterns and stand a chance of building up a good enough relationship.

13.

Adult, Child and Parent

One of the stranger but more useful suggestions of psychotherapy – and, in particular, a branch of it known as 'transactional analysis' – is that all of us contain within ourselves three essential personalities:

- a child
- a parent
- an adult

To flesh these out a little:

The *child* is typically vulnerable, touching, trusting, weak, in need, incapable of properly looking after themselves and crying out for assistance, tenderness, support, structure and some rules.

For their part, the *parent* is strong, dominant, in control, responsible but also often chiding, critical, hectoring – and busy from all their cares and duties.

Meanwhile the *adult* is sane, thoughtful, in command, neither too weak nor too strong, creative and kind.

In an ideal world, we would all be able to toggle between these three personality types with relative ease. In a good relationship, we would constantly be moving between all three roles in ourselves, mostly hovering in the adult zone, but able – when occasion demands – to go into parent or child mode.

For example, when we are feeling sad and under pressure, it should be part of health to know how to become a child again, to show our need, ask for help, curl into a ball, become small and trust that we can be met with kindness and sympathy without fearing attack or belittlement.

Then again, there should also be moments in a relationship, particularly when our usually adult partner has hit a crisis and descended into a child-like mode when we are powerfully able to step up into a parental role and become ministering, indulgent to weakness and tantrums, calm in the face of irrationality and secure enough in ourselves to know that the child-like partner will in a little while revert back to the maturity and self-command that we typically expect from them.

If a couple have small children, then for long stretches both may need to act as parent, but then once the kids are in bed, they might both have a go at being sweet, slightly naughty children, or one might play adult to the other one's needy younger self.

The difficulty – for couples and individuals – is when people get stuck in particular positions, when they can only ever be children, or only ever parents or only ever adults. There are relationships where, for example, one partner is always the child and the other is always the parent. One person is forever being a bit irresponsible, a bit naughty; they leave their clothes everywhere, they don't book in for a driving lesson, they don't go to the dry-cleaner's, they forget to do the shopping and they lose the keys. They can be highly endearing – when one is in the mood – but you'd hesitate a lot before leaving them in charge. And on the other side of the ledger there is a parental-type partner who is always chiding and reminding the child what to do, who is super competent, forever rather stressed, alternately indulgent to the child but also on the edge of being cross and punitive.

Associated with this can be a deep reluctance on the part of the parental figure ever to access their child self. They always have to be strong; they always have to be mother or father; they cannot go anywhere near being little. They have only disdain for anything vulnerable or seemingly fragile. Everyone says that they cope so well, whatever the situation – but that's precisely the problem. No one who really copes well copes all the time. Breaking down and being a helpless, defenceless infant belongs to healthy adulthood. There is no such thing as maturity without a constant connection with the immature self from which one has emerged.

Why, we might ask, do people – and therefore couples – get stuck in these roles? Why can it be so hard to move? Why are some people rigidly incapable of feeling their way into the role of child, parent or adult? In all cases, we are – typically – looking at something in the past that has made an easy transition to a particular position untenable or frightening.

There are people stuck in the child role for whom adulthood and parenthood present insuperable difficulties. Perhaps they are the offspring of a loving parent who couldn't tolerate their own nascent maturity: to be deemed worthy of love, they had to stay baby. However much they might have wished to grow up, they know deep in their unconscious that love and care will only ever be available if they fall into line and continue to be who they substantially were when they were 5, at an emotional level at least. They can either have love or they can have an adulthood – but they cannot have both; such is the cruel stricture under which some of us grow up. They might have been parented by a child-like parent – themselves irresponsible or immature, frightened of sex or unable to fully inhabit the adult world – to whom they had to show unhelpful loyalty, probably because there was no one else in the vicinity who could be at once loving and in command of fully adult capacities.

Or else, one may feel one has to stay stuck in the child mode because a parent would be angry, castrating and humiliating if one dared to show independence and pride in one's adult ideals. Perhaps a parent was so rivalrous and envious that we learnt to sabotage our potential to be competent and confident so as not to incur murderous jealousy. We chose life over the danger of being cut down by a vengeful, insecure caregiver, but at a price.

At the other end of the spectrum, very poignantly, there are people whose younger selves were so badly treated, who experienced such anxiety and lack of support when they were children that the idea of being small, even for a few hours, presents unbearable challenges to their integrity. They may be very happy playing mummy and daddy; they cannot be baby. The very idea sickens them and makes them bristle – though, tragically, they don't even realise what is going on and certainly can't connect their nausea with the difficulties of their past.

The route out of all these impasses is, as always, self-exploration and mutual honesty between couples. As we embark on any relationship, we should wonder whether one of these three roles – child, parent or adult – might present an especially difficult prospect (we should pick up on the inner wince or recoil when the thought comes up). And if it does, we should then have the courage to admit as much to our partner; to say, with self-deprecation and calm, that – though we know it might be important to do so – we really have a bit of a problem around being child, parent or adult, but are committed to finding out more.

Problems are never as bad as they might be once we get them into consciousness and circulate them in discussion. To admit to being a child who doesn't dare to be an adult, or a parent who doesn't dare to be a child isn't just a peculiar-sounding confession. It suggests the presence of someone profoundly committed to eventual maturity and on their way to being the best kind of grown-up.

14.

Beyond Mind-reading

Of course, we don't officially have the slightest belief in mind-reading; we scoff at the absurd idea that we might telepathically know what number between one and a million a stranger is thinking of, or that we could place our hands on someone else's skull and thereby intuit the precise details of what they dreamt last night. But in relationships, whatever our professed scepticism, we very frequently proceed as if mind-reading were not only possible but a standard requirement and possibility in love – something the absence of which we would have every right to complain about with bitterness and surprise. In a great many ways, we simply assume that our partner must automatically be able to know the movements and preoccupations of our minds. And our expectations show up in one of the standard ways in which we speak of the perfection of a lover in the initial days of rapture: they seem to know what we are thinking, *without us needing to speak* …

But our superstitious commitment to mind-reading soon evolves into something darker as relationships proceed; for example, when:

- We get huffy that our partner didn't realise that our off-colour comment was only a joke.
- We can't imagine they could even think we'd like the bizarre birthday present they bought us.
- We're offended that they like a book we've already decided is silly.
- We're annoyed that they didn't know we wouldn't want to go to the mountains this summer.
- They can't understand the mood we are in when we get back from having lunch with our mother.

We get worked up because we can't conceive that certain ideas and feelings that are so vivid in our minds should not immediately be obvious to someone who professes to care for us. We quickly fall into believing that the partner's incomprehension can only be explained in one way: it must come down to wilfulness or nastiness. And, therefore, it seems only fair that we respond with one of our standard forms of punishment due to all those who should have known better: a sulk – that paradoxical pattern of behaviour in which we refuse, for several hours or even a day or two, to reveal what is wrong to our confused partner *because they should just know*.

The origins of our reckless hopes are, in a sense, extremely touching. When we were little a parent really did, at key moments, seem to know what we were thinking without us needing to speak. As if by magic, they guessed that we might want some milk. With a medium's genius, they determined that we needed a bath or a nap or that a blanket was a bit scratchy for our cheek. And from this, an equation formed in our minds: *Whenever I am properly loved, I do not need to explain.*

But however great our parents were at reading our minds, they had a huge advantage over our partners: we were – back then – really very simple. Our requirements were usefully few: we needed only to be fed, bathed, put to bed and entertained with a picture book or bit of string. We had no advanced views on politics, no complicated opinions on interior design; our psyches didn't register faint tremors of sarcasm or hypocrisy; we couldn't be thrown off course by the pronunciation of a word.

How much more complicated we have grown since then. We are now adults who can feel very strongly that a table must be placed symmetrically in a room twenty centimetres from the door to the kitchen; or we like it very much when our partner rolls up their sleeves, but we hate them wearing a short-sleeved shirt, especially the green one; we like being teased (but only sometimes and never about our age); we are very critical of our mother but can't allow anyone to mention her habit of being late; we come across as confident but think of ourselves as shy;

we like art but have an aversion to museums; we love stone fruits but hate peaches; we talk a lot about politics but can't stand reading newspapers. Our partner's inability to know all this – fast and decisively – necessarily feels like an intimate insult, and the complex task of explaining our thoughts and attitudes like an unreasonable imposition.

But once we accept that there is no such thing as mind-reading, a central part of our relationship becomes the slow, careful process of piecing together – in one another's company – what matters to us and why, with all the surprise and moments of genuine revelation this entails. We accept that there will be an immense amount we need to teach each other about who we are pretty much every day – while trusting that this is not an attack on the idea of love.

There's another slightly more subtle manifestation of our misplaced faith in mind-reading: we too often assume that we only ever need to explain things once to people. With fatal generosity, we credit our partner with immense powers of absorption and retention. And then we're shocked and hurt when it turns out that despite having mentioned it three months ago, they still don't seem to realise that a car door does not need to be slammed shut, that leaving a small tip at the cafe is worse than leaving none at all, or that our cousin is, in our view, secretly jealous of us. 'How can you not know that?' we irritably ask. 'I told you before.'

Instead, we should embrace the intelligent pessimism of religions: they never imagine that being told once that Allah is great or that we really ought to be more forgiving of our enemies could possibly suffice. We need to be told everything multiple times – perhaps every day, even five times a day, depending on the faith. Religions know that the human mind is inherently leaky: a big, important message may be received and understood in the moment, but its shelf life is bound to be short; this isn't any special failing on the part of an individual, it's the natural lot of the species. Explanations and exhortations therefore need to be endlessly repeated – and to resent this is to go to war with psychological reality.

To give up on mind-reading in its various guises means starting, at last, a new and deeper phase of a union, one in which patient self-explanation is given a rightful place in the ongoing noble project of coming to understand, and properly love, another person.

Exercise

To begin the patient task of undoing our mind-reading assumptions, consider the following:

1. What do you feel your partner should really already know about your sensitivities given how long you've been together? Make a list that features such details as: interior design, their family, travel arrangements, friendships, politics, your family, shoes, the bathroom ...

2. Now go and see the partner and ask them to go through the items and explore how much they really do know. Correct any shortfalls in knowledge with patience and humour.

3. Repeat the exercise the other way.

15.

Resentment

There is no worse enemy of love than resentment, because we don't usually notice its presence or realise its power. Resentment starts as anger against a lover that, out of modesty or pride, we neither properly acknowledge to ourselves nor cleanly express to our partner. We seethe, but privately and unknowingly, and as a consequence we fall prey to depression, moodiness and a lack of desire.

At the core of the problem is the fact that resentments tend to be generated by what can look – from the outside – like absurdly small factors. We don't notice how annoyed we are and then hold back from 'making a fuss' with someone we still long to appear impressive in front of. We suffer in silence because we operate with a hugely inadequate picture of what we're allowed to be upset by, and yet we get upset all the same – only more so and without a chance of catharsis.

We would need a very attentive documentary team to catch resentments as they build. Our partner might say only 'hmm' when we mention that we are worried about a situation at work. Or they might get a little too excited at the prospect of meeting up with an old friend, when they are rarely pleased to meet anyone we introduce them to. Or they might buy a piece of clothing without asking us what we think – unlike the concern they used to show for our views on their wardrobe in the early days.

Few of us are ever completely sure of whether we matter solidly to the partner we depend on. Doubts constantly creep in – often fuelled by the vagaries and pains of our early lives. Love's survival can rarely, in our deep minds, be entirely assured. But we know too that we cannot be 'childish', that we should not whine and that no one likes a needy person.

Yet the trouble with small resentments is that, like a constant drip of water onto granite, they can eventually bore into the centre of our minds. Just as our bodies may be immensely sensitive to trace amounts of certain substances (a minute quantity of strychnine will kill us almost at once), so our minds can be conclusively offended by a missing smile or a tiny delay before a greeting. And yet not only are we infinitely sensitive, we refuse properly to accept the extent to which we might be so.

The idea that little details can need, and deserve, careful attention is one that we have no trouble recognising in certain privileged areas of life. We will go along with a musician who agonises for weeks about the exact nature of the percussion during a chorus and gets very upset when, in the final version, it's not exactly as they had wished. We have no difficulty in appreciating that, during a screening of a new film, a director might want to suggest tiny variations in sequencing and pace in order to make a closing scene more effective. We allow a poet to spend hours wondering if a specific word is right for a particular line; an interior designer will be praised for worrying about the precise hang and fall of the folds in a curtain. We don't think any of these people are being fussy or over-intense. Indeed, we may acclaim them as geniuses for picking up so well on details that coarser minds might overlook.

However, when we come to something no less important – the success or failure of love – we lose confidence in the entire concept of details being worthy of time, consideration, intelligent discussion and (perhaps) adjustment. Instead, we accuse ourselves of 'making a big deal about nothing' and worry we might be whining.

An ideal session of resentment analysis would make it clear that we were discussing only details, while nevertheless acknowledging that details can matter a lot. There would be a sense that much might be going very well in a couple but, like the film director in the cutting room or the musician in the studio, we are giving ourselves a chance to focus in on details, not in order to create problems, but to ensure that small ones don't metastasise. We would try to get as accurate as possible in explaining why a detail happened to matter to us. We would concede that there was probably nothing inherently awful about a given trigger – for example, the partner's love of whistling or their passion for yoga. Other people would evidently have no problem with these things. We would then try to lay bare the personal story behind our specific antipathies.

Typically, the communicative error we make is to elaborate on *how much* we dislike something rather than *why* we do so. We say something is vulgar, ghastly, appalling or stupid, but this only intensifies, rather than resolves, conflict. What we should invariably strive to do is explain the origins of our distastes with particular reference to our fears, for fears are always a lot nicer to hear about than hates.

Doing so will force us to dig into our minds. Where is our sensitivity rooted? What bits of our pasts are being engaged? With whistling, the sound might give us the impression that our partner thinks they are alone in our presence; hearing them whistle, we feel as if we have temporarily been shut out of their existence – an idea that might feel especially painful because of the way we were handled in childhood by an erratic and often absent parent. Or the partner's taste for yoga might evoke in us a picture of woolliness and disinterest in practical matters, which, on account of difficulties we suffered around money when we were young, might set off wildly inaccurate but frightening images of chaos and penury.

By tracing irritants back to personal fears, we stop them acquiring a moral dimension in our minds: they are about us and our vulnerabilities; they are not universal truths that we can pontificate on. We take responsibility for what annoys us, and at the same time we share our discomforts before they can build up into fully fledged arguments against the person we are trying very hard to love.

Exercise

1. Let yourself be as finickety as a music critic or as particular as an interior designer. What little details of your partner's behaviour grate on you? Make the longest, most detailed list you can, covering issues like routines, timekeeping, levels of cleanliness, varieties of laughter and taste in socks, childhood friends and breakfast cereals.

2. Go through the list and try to explain why these things bother you, with reference to your past. Be as explicit as possible: what is it in your history that has been offended by these often unobtrusive ideas and behaviours?

3. Suggest that your partner make, very nicely, the same kind of complaints against you, for things that you could not easily have imagined would upset them. Ask them to explain what parts of their history are being engaged: how are you 'frightening' them?

16.

Good Listening

We have it drummed into us from an early stage that good relationships rely on both partners spending a lot of time listening to one another. As a result, almost all lovers feel in their hearts, with perhaps a touch of weariness, that they have put in a good number of hours listening to their companions: their stories, their pet schemes, their views on the world, their particular irritations with this or that facet of existence ... And yet, despite both a theoretical respect for the idea of listening and all the many occasions when we have technically been taking in what our partners have been telling us, there is still nothing more common than for people in relationships to report feeling that they have not been *properly* listened to. *Feeling* heard is evidently a good deal more complicated than *being* heard.

What, then, does it mean to listen to someone properly? Here are a few features of good listening:

A good listener doesn't correct exaggerations

It's a rookie error of the poor listener to try to intervene in a partner's dialogue in order to introduce perspective and nuance, on the basis that this should at all times be present in order for a conversation to flow well. When the partner says that their colleague is 'a complete tosshead who understands nothing at all', the poor listener might add that this is 'a bit of an exaggeration' because they were pretty good – all told – in their work at the recent conference. Or the partner will accuse their father of understanding 'not a damn thing about anything' and the bad listener will bring up that he was fairly good with the neighbours the time they lost the keys.

The normal rules of conversation certainly suggest that we should clearly announce our doubts and disagreements with what another person is saying in order to maintain our integrity and standing. But this is to misunderstand what a lot of conversation in relationships is actually about. Our partners are at key moments not asking for precise corroboration of what they are saying. They don't want to get to a scientifically verifiable truth. They want us to enter into the spirit rather than the letter of a specific frustration, disappointment or outrage that is tearing at them. Whether or not they are completely right to be feeling a certain way is secondary. What counts is that they do not, at a moment of considerable distress, want to be alone with their pain.

Good listeners don't set conditions for listening

Many of us, when we are being asked for our attention by a partner, promise to give it to them wholeheartedly – but on certain conditions. We say that we will promise to listen to them, *but only if they calm down*. Or *if they decide to be logical*. Or *if they stop shouting*. The request almost makes sense. If one was in a courtroom, a stern judge might well level the same requirements. But this demand for a soft voice, a calm manner and a completely steady mind slyly evades why such ingredients are missing in the first place: the scale of our annoyance with the person we are trying to get through to. To be not only not listened to but also then told that one will never be listened to until the reasons why one can't speak with utter calm have been addressed becomes a major irritant of its own.

A good listener listens through a storm, even when they are being verbally attacked, even when the partner doesn't quite make sense, even when they've just been called a muttonhead or a cock – and they do so because they keep one key ingredient in mind: the reason why the partner is behaving so unreasonably is fear, and beneath that, love. They are terrified that they have grown dependent on someone who seems, at that moment, to be in some way very unkind, very blocked and very uncomprehending. This may not be true, but this is how it feels and it is the cause of great fear. To up this fear further by insisting on total serenity before a chat can begin is to pour acid into a wound. Good listeners may not *want* to listen to tantrums, but in the end they do, because they understand very well, and have compassion for, the underlying panicked love that powers them.

Good listeners keep listening

A standard rule of conversation suggests that when one person says something, we should come back with an anecdote of our own that matches what has just been shared. A friend complains about their boss, so we complain about ours; a colleague had a blocked drain at home, so did our sister.

But with a partner we need to put this social convention firmly to one side. They don't need us to match or top their problem. They just want us to acknowledge the unique, particular nature of their troubles. Instead of interrupting and diverting, we should perpetually go in for encouragement; we should in effect always be saying: 'Tell me more.'

Good listening isn't literal

What a person wants us to hear is seldom exactly what they have said. Think of a frustrated child who says they want to 'kill their teacher'. We know that they aren't hatching a murderous plot, they are just finding the most charged terms in which to express how frustrated they feel with someone who dominates their days and ruins their chances of having fun.

The same applies to a partner's more extreme statements. They may, at an instant of maximum distress, say that they hate us, that they wish they'd never met us and that we have ruined their entire lives. It may seem trite to point this out, but almost always – if we are lucky – this is not quite what they mean. Their actual intent lies somewhat to the side of the actual words they are using.

What they say	What they mean
I hate you.	Reassure me that you still love me.
I loathe my job.	I worry I'm not good enough at the career I've chosen.
I don't care if I see you on Saturday night or not.	Tell me you want to see me.

The true meaning has been skirted because it is too raw, too revealing and – most often – too vulnerable. It is never easy to accept how much we rely on someone we cannot control. Good listeners know they must translate from an indirect to a direct idiom – gifting their partners the intense, touching and dependent words that they have not yet had the courage to find.

Proper listening isn't a natural accomplishment, it's just incredibly nice. It is an act of the greatest kindness – a true expression of love – to allow a partner to be right when they are wrong, to lament the conduct of others when it's partly their fault and to be volubly miserable around things that, in reality, aren't necessarily so tragic. To listen to this means that we are attending to the subtle, complex and very real intricacies of another's life. And secretly we hope that someone will, one day, love us enough to do the same for us.

Exercise

Imagine the nicest, most generous interpretations of what a partner might mean when they say the following:

What they say	What they mean
You're not making enough money.	
You don't like the way I look.	
You never think about me.	
I can't stand your friends.	
You're turning into your mother/father.	

17.

Diplomacy

Being 'diplomatic' doesn't sit at all well with our current ideas of what a good relationship should be like; the term sounds fake, hesitant and musty. We like to imagine couples who are always open and frank with one another, who can say directly what they think and feel – whereas the diplomat is someone who softens or bends their words. They'll say a situation is 'tricky' when bombs are exploding or talk of a 'strained friendship' in the wake of an attempted assassination. They're rarely totally honest – they will warmly shake hands with enemies and go to parties with people they privately despise. They can frequently invite accusations of hypocrisy.

But to give the diplomat their due, they operate with a rare and interesting sense of priorities. They care first and foremost about results. They want the other to understand something, but they know that declaring intentions may not be the best way to realise them.

The diplomat operates with a pessimistic picture of the mind. They think of it as a kind of defensive fortress that is set up constantly to repel unwelcome truths. To angrily tell the leader of a hostile nation that they are being stupid and reckless may be to state a truth; but the diplomat knows a tyrant is very unlikely to absorb such a statement calmly, think it through and say: 'Oh yes, on reflection, I see you do have a point. What do you think I need to do to improve?'

The diplomat is interested in the careful ways in which a truth may need to be presented in order to take up residence in the mind of an averagely confused, agitated and passionate person. Likewise, in the context of a relationship, the diplomatic lover might hold off expressing any of their frustration the moment it occurs in the kitchen past midnight. They will wait until the next day when everyone is rested. They might lay on layers of flattery, they will ask a leading question rather than make a direct accusation and they will couch their assertions in the weaker language of 'maybe', 'perhaps' and 'possibly'. This is not at all because they are pathetic, hugely accommodating or conflict-avoidant; it is just that they are particularly determined to get messages through to their partner and are devoted to a realistic theory of how they might succeed.

A key technique of the diplomat–partner is that they try very hard to define what the problem afflicting the couple really is. Emotionally we often totalise: when we get upset, we feel our lover is globally awful, everything about them is horrible – and if emotion could speak directly, it would say: 'I hate you, this whole relationship is miserable.' The diplomat, by contrast, focuses on the specific causes of trouble. It isn't remotely 'everything' that is ever really likely to be the problem. By searching for the actual issue, the diplomat can specify a target rather than declare a war.

A second big idea the diplomat embraces is that negotiations might reasonably take some time. They have a sense of how hard it is for the other person to properly embrace any unwelcome idea – and they know that the ground has to be prepared, the issue has to be raised gently at first and accommodation must be made for pushback. But none of this is fatal; they will just take a slightly different tack and keep going. They might be at this for many months. The most distinctive thing about the diplomat is that they are, in the end, hopeful: they are motivated by the idea that a good outcome can be found through the stealthy exercise of their craft.

It is open to us all to practise our diplomatic skills via specific exercises that encourage kindly and productive indirectness.

Rather than being merely sly or underhand, being diplomatic is an act of love; it means generously and kindly attempting to help someone over an incapacity without drawing attention to what we are doing. It is an open-hearted move that knows we all need assistance with the truth and don't deserve censure for our defences (the person who denies that they ever reject unwelcome truths is only defending themselves against an unwelcome truth). We should proudly be indirect with our partners because there is something extremely direct and honest that we long to do with them through our tentative language: help them grow.

What we might feel	What we might diplomatically say
You don't give a shit about anyone but yourself.	I was wondering whether you sometimes lose interest in what I am saying.
You're so disorganised, you'll never get your career off the ground.	It might be worth trying to think more about priorities.
That jumper is revolting on you.	Burgundy doesn't quite do you justice.

Exercise

Think of diplomatic ways to express some of what you might be feeling:

What we might feel	What we might diplomatically say

18.

Sexual Expectations

There's an appealing but tragically unhelpful myth about sex and relationships: once we find the right partner, our sex life will be complete. We'll at last settle into a comfortable, reliable (and sometimes very exciting) rhythm of good sex with someone we love who loves us back.

But in reality, getting together with someone long term is often the start of new and uncomfortable troubles around sex. Over time, three basic areas of distress can emerge:

- There's something that we really want to do in bed but we feel we can't possibly ask our partner.
- One of us has been unfaithful.
- We rarely, if ever, have sex now.

There's such an emphasis on being 'good in bed' that it can feel shameful and agonising even to raise these matters with our partner (let alone with a friend), but in braver moments we can look squarely at our pains and constructively consider how we might address them. To take them one by one:

There's something we really want to do in bed but
we feel we can't possibly ask our partner

With unfortunate encouragement from our societies, friendship groups and upbringing, we develop the idea that there are certain specific ways to get respectably excited in bed – and that there are, by contrast, a hinterland of 'taboo' fantasies that only hugely weird or sick people would ever find thrilling.

But because something in this taboo area excites us nevertheless, we may have a constant anxiety around how our partner would react were we to be honest. We anticipate humiliation and rejection from the person who knows us best at a moment of maximal supposed authenticity. And so sex (however good it may be in other respects) can become an arena of pain, shame and sullen anger.

The solution is to burn a fundamental truth into our minds: sexual desire is inherently strange and we are not responsible for any of its oddities (the only caveat being that we mustn't hurt any unconsenting people with our wants). The idea of there being a limited 'good' way of having sex is a local, recent (and very unkind) invention – not a reflection of reality. The person who insists that only 'normal' sex is acceptable isn't an ideal representative of sanity; they are almost certainly someone in denial about their own more deeply hidden, but equally exotic, fantasies.

What we have to keep in mind – when we falter in the face of admitting a desire to our partner – is that there is a very reasonable and standard story to be told about why we have ended up with the particular kink we have. We need first to trace that story for ourselves, piecing it together in sympathetic steps from childhood onwards – and then dare to tell our partners without shame or judgement. This is just who we are, for better and for worse.

We should introduce our partner to the less familiar zones of our excitement not when we are actually in bed with them and urgently wanting to do something – the point of maximal urgency is, strategically, the least suitable moment for revelation – but at a time when we can interest them in the story of our life.

One of us has been unfaithful

The words 'unfaithful' and 'betrayal' carry such negative weight that anyone who has ever been their victim is advised at once to leave, to preserve their dignity and to honour modern values.

Infidelity, however, covers a wide range of very different scenarios, and what a sexual act outside a relationship actually truly means depends on a specific emotional context we would be wise to explore before calling time on any couple.

One tricky possibility is that the unfaithful one was not primarily interested in sex at all; what they really wanted was to be liked, talked and listened to – their need was primarily emotional. This does not mean that all in the couple is well, it just places a different spin on where the problem lies and what the possible solution to it might be. It won't be sterilisation or a prison that is called for, but – maybe – a chance to explore why channels of feeling have become blocked. Though it is the sex component that, once an affair is revealed, typically gets all the outraged attention, the straying lover might have been using sex to communicate – badly but genuinely – a more poignant truth: that they felt abandoned. They were attempting – in a mangled and misguided way – to make a plea to their partner for love.

In other words, a 'betrayal' isn't always and necessarily a rejection of an existing relationship; it can on occasion represent an incompetent but real attempt to repair it. The ideal response to such a discovery wouldn't be to declare the relationship over, but to try to work out *why* what happened happened and how the wound could appropriately be tended to.

This is not a strayer's charter, just a reminder that there is space for a form of understanding that can turn an act of infidelity (massively unwelcome and hurtful though it might be) from an outrage and a monstrosity into something we can at least understand, unpick and perhaps even survive.

We rarely, if ever, have sex now

One of the standard things we might hear, when someone explains to us why they left their partner is that 'we hadn't had sex for years'. The plea picks up on the basic notion that a key sign of the health and viability of any relationship lies in the frequency of sexual contact between its participants. The end of sex must therefore legitimately and necessarily signal the end of love.

But if we lift the lid on what sex actually means, we might conclude something a little different. Suppose we ask the bizarre-sounding question: why do we actually want sex? The ordinary answer is that we want it for pleasure and excitement. But this might not, in fact, be very accurate about our needs. There are lots of sources of pleasure (and, indelicately but honestly, we can note that masturbation can be very pleasurable, too). A less familiar but deeper answer may be that really, via sex, we are seeking proof of affection and enthusiasm. When we're rebuffed sexually, the pain isn't just that we won't be having an orgasm with a person, it's that we are being given a sense that they don't particularly like us. The sting is to our sense of lovability rather than just to our nerve endings.

So we could say that under the surface of bitterness about sex, it's never strictly only how much sex is going on that matters, but how much affection, tenderness, interest and warmth is being demonstrated. Sex is operating as a proxy measure, but it's not in itself the thing that truly counts. We could easily imagine having a lot of sex without love – and suffering because of it. Or being loved deeply but for whatever reason not having much sex – and being content.

This helps us to put a more accurate finger on when a lack of sex should realistically become a matter for dissent or a parting of ways. Insofar as an absence of sex is independent of any shortfall in love, we should stay. Insofar as it is further evidence of a decline and absence of love, we could be following the logic of the heart to leave.

Exercise

1.   Name a 'weird' sexual desire you have (if only in your mind).

2.   Outline in as much detail as possible the steps and stages by which this desire evolved in you.

3.   How might you explain this desire to a partner?

4.   If there has been an affair, the straying partner should explain their motivations. To what extent did this infidelity come about from a fruitless attempt to complain about a shortfall in affection from the betrayed person?

5.   How else might you feel that affection and tenderness could be offered other than via sex?

6.   It may not be your fantasy ideal, but how could you perhaps – to your surprise – manage really quite well in a sexless relationship so long as there was a plentiful supply of certain other things as well? What would these things need to be? Are they present now?

19.

Beyond Standard Relationships

There's a collective picture of what a good relationship is supposed to look like that's become deeply embedded in our imaginations. Let's call it the Standard Model and imagine some of what it requires of a proper couple:

- to share a home and always sleep in the same bed
- to only ever have sex with one another
- to share all domestic tasks
- to merge finances
- to get very involved in each other's families
- to have children
- to share the same group of friends
- to spend nearly every evening and weekend together
- to always take holidays together

Because this picture is so familiar today – and so prestigious – we don't easily get round to asking if it's always a very good arrangement and, in particular, whether it's a particularly good arrangement for us, given who we are and all the many ways in which we are fastidious, unique and peculiar.

The Standard Model totalises

To get a perspective on one drawback of the Standard Model, we can try a thought experiment. Imagine a society that's long been devoted to a sporting event in which every competitor has to run a race, then lift some weights, swim, do the pole vault, ride a horse, last five rounds in a boxing ring and finally scale a climbing wall. It's not considered proper to do any of these things *separately*; everyone must do all of them.

To outside observers, this might seem a hugely bizarre system: why don't they just let people choose which bit, or bits, they want to specialise in? Why should wanting to swim entail entering the boxing ring? Similar questions could be raised of the Standard Model of relationships and its multiple, interconnected requirements. Why should sharing domestic tasks involve sleeping in the same bed? Why should merging finances be twinned with going on holiday together?

To help us notice our own tastes, we might go through the different elements combined in the Standard Model, one by one, and privately rate how significant each one might actually be to us.

Activity	Not important	Could be important	Definitely important
Always sleeping in the same bed			
Sharing all domestic tasks absolutely equally			
Spending nearly every evening and every weekend together			
Having children			
Holidaying together			
Being sexually exclusive			

If we haven't been able to tick every entry in the 'definitely important' column, we are on the way to being a Standard Model rebel. Thought-provokingly, a great many of us already are.

The Standard Model doesn't acknowledge trade-offs

The Standard Model insinuates a particular image of closeness. But it leaves a great many elements out and doesn't square up to trade-offs. It doesn't acknowledge that two people might well get on better if they sometimes had time apart. It doesn't allow that getting very involved with a partner's family might be a major emotional burden that undermines goodwill elsewhere, or even simply that sharing a bed might lead to disrupted sleep patterns and consequent grumpiness. In particular, it fails to come clean about the vast costs to a relationship of having children. The immense emotional investment in raising a family almost always – in time – radically diminishes the pleasure that two people can take in each other's company. One can have intimacy or children, but rarely both – at least for many years.

The Standard Model invites us to clarify our priorities. With its example in mind, we can ask: are we more focused on having a love relationship with our partner, or is having a family the main thing for us? Does sex matter, or is an absence of every jealous feeling a bigger priority? We have for too long suffered because we have not dared to look at the trade-offs that exist, and yet we were making them anyway given that perfection and holistic joy have never been on the cards. We would significantly help ourselves if we could at least consciously understand what we were sacrificing and in the name of what advantage.

It would make a great difference if, in practice, we could sit down very early on with a partner with whom things were starting to go well and try to define for ourselves as individuals and together as a couple what we actually want from a union. What are we hoping and trying to do together? It's a challenging and essential question that the Standard Model unfairly renders illegitimate. Naively, it can seem as if the only possible answer for a decent and kind person would be: 'We should do *everything* together.'

Yet a truly accurate (and therefore properly loving) answer would have to be more flavoured. We can imagine what some honest responses from different people might look like if they had bravely explored their minds and constructed authentic lives for themselves as a result:

In our relationship, we see each other for dinner twice a week, we have some shared finances and we go on one big holiday together each year. We've never had sex with each other.

We both need a lot of personal space, so although we live in the same flat, we've got pretty strictly demarcated areas. I'd never go into my partner's room unless they specifically asked me in. When we have sex it's usually on the sofa bed in the sitting room. We each make a contribution to shared expenses, but other than that our finances are completely separate. We always take our holidays separately.

We have two children and collaborate very deeply and lovingly around caring for and educating them, but we only live together at weekends.

We share a home and a bed, we're sexually faithful to one another, but apart from that our lives are rather separate. We have very different friendship groups and interests; we rarely spend an evening together, but it means a lot to be back home at eleven for a kiss and a glass of wine.

We are in constant contact, we see each other every day, we are devoted to each other sexually, but we've discovered we simply cannot share a house; we'd drive each other mad.

To familiarise ourselves with the range of good living arrangements that couples have discovered is to liberate ourselves from the oppressive power of the Standard Model: this may be perfect for some people but evidently equally crushing for a great many others. This entails a thrilling, slightly terrifying realisation: there is in reality no particular reason why we have to do things a certain way. It's up to us to create for ourselves and our partner a vision of coupledom that – however eccentric it might seem at first glance – allows us to do very well the one thing we all really want: to be happy together.

20.

Endings Don't Have to Be Tragedies

One of the greatest enemies of successful relationships is the often immensely well-intended inertia that keeps us lingering, and emotionally dying, in unsuccessful ones. But we'll never get into a good relationship if we can't or don't want to get out of a bad one. Why do we, then, so often stay stuck? A range of reasons present themselves.

The first has to do with a frequent refusal to accept that love has died. In order to escape this hugely awkward thought, we tell ourselves a half-truth that can keep couples going for years: we do love the partner, we say, we just want them to change. A lot. In many areas. Seeking change sounds a lot more respectable than no longer loving – and the union can thereby be kept alive at least until the children are fully grown. But if maintaining a relationship involves us having to vow to become a totally different version of ourselves, we might start to wonder. The question that should start to dawn upon us is: *Do we actually belong together?* It's a little as if our partner had bought a dog and then condemned it for barking. Shame can get in the way of seeing something obvious: we have outgrown one another.

We also stay for too long because we get immensely skilled at telling ourselves happy stories about the future; we may have acquired the technique during an interminable and sad childhood. We know how to calm our partner down; we are adept at tiptoeing round their moods; we look forward to next year and the year after. We sidestep confrontations; we tell ourselves that, if only we try hard enough, things will get better in a while. We are so good at enduring strife, we end up feeling that this is what a relationship should be like: a state where the good things will always be just over the horizon and where the possibility of warmth and empathy is continually deferred. What we're struggling to acknowledge is that our faith in what lies 'over the horizon' is ultimately a neurosis in our deep minds. Hope can become responsible for the most hopeless situations.

At other times, it is a fear of hurting our partner that prevents us from leaving. We don't love them any more, but nor can we bear to see them upset, so we might be willing to stay at least until New Year – or maybe even next spring or summer – to avoid a devastating scene. Yet whatever we like to tell ourselves, we are already hurting them a great deal by remaining beside them simply because of the pain it would cause us to see them crying. We are using up some of the best years of their lives because we are not brave enough to endure a few hours of discomfort. This isn't kindness or consideration; it's desperate cowardice dressed up as compassion. Of course we don't want to hurt our partner. But that's not the issue. Our ultimate responsibility is to the rest of their lives, which we will continue to destroy until we have had the kindness to find our tongue.

If we've got children together, the hesitation can come from another direction. Children almost always wish their parents could stay together, but analysed a little more closely, what they really wish is more nuanced. We might conceive of children as essentially deeply practical creatures, comparable in many ways to guests who have decided to spend their holidays in a particular hotel under a certain management, of whom they've grown very used and (usually) very fond. What these guests want above all is to secure a set of deeply pragmatic and very understandable goals:

- They want a minimum of administrative hassle.
- They want the adults around them to get on cheerfully.
- They want as little alteration in routine as possible.
- They don't want to be made to hang out with new people.
- They don't want to meet a half-naked adult stranger at breakfast.
- They don't want rumours to circulate about their 'hotel' that will make them look weird in front of their peers.

That said, they arguably don't particularly care about a whole host of other things:

- how often, or how pleasingly, their parents are having sex
- whether their parents are the deepest sorts of soulmates
- what their parents get up to in their spare time

These comparative lists start to suggest a possible answer to the dilemma of whether one might stay or leave insofar as the welfare of children is the issue. The question can be answered either way. Both staying and leaving could be made profoundly compatible with children's concerns, because the emotional satisfaction of their parents isn't the central issue for young people. The central issue is how much disruption there might be in their lives. There are ways of staying that will cause massive disruptions: horrific fights between the hotel managers that won't allow guests to enjoy very much of their time. And there are ways of leaving that also create extreme disruption, or ways that stir up almost no disruption at all ... The reason the stay-or-leave question is so tricky – in essence – is that children don't really care whether you stay or leave; they want an undisturbed life, a pleasant atmosphere and a good mood among the management, which could be compatible or incompatible with either choice. It just depends how it's done.

For those who might want to leave, one can imagine conceiving of a range of innovations:

- Perhaps the children wouldn't move between homes, the parents would.
- Perhaps the children wouldn't hang out a lot with new partners, just the parents would.
- Perhaps the children wouldn't have to know about the depths of the disappointment between the parents, they'd just notice a sensible and kindly relationship between them.

A concern for more authentic and emotionally alive relationships has been, in many ways, an enormous advance for humanity. But it's left us very confused as to what the priorities are for children. A non-Romantic worldview provides a clear answer: one doesn't need to spend the rest of one's life with someone with whom one no longer connects 'for the sake of the children'. But at the same time, one must ensure that if one leaves, everything is done to keep the practical basis of a child's life as stable as possible – as with a hotel that has come under new, divided ownership but bends over backwards to make sure its guests suffer few inconveniences.

Lastly, we don't leave because, in many societies, the vision of a good relationship is that it should end only in death. It's a moving but inherently odd notion. In some areas, we can accept that good undertakings are allowed to have endings; we don't blame a novel for having a final chapter or an opera a closing scene. It would be immensely helpful to import this artistic perspective into our romantic lives. A relationship that finishes needn't have been a failure; it may (like *War and Peace* or *Così fan tutte*) have been *completed*: it accomplished its task, it arrived at its destiny, it fulfilled its potential. We did together what it was in our power to do.

Relationships should logically conclude when we've learnt as much from a partner as we'll ever be able to; when we've absorbed so much through being with them that we're now ready to take our leave and perhaps – as it were – attend a school with a new teacher. One of the kindest and truest views of relationships is that they are in effect schools for emotional growth – which also implies that we can legitimately graduate from them. We can leave not because we hate our partner but because we've completed the course they can offer. There's a parallel in the way that parents can be pleased that their child leaves home – not because they are glad to see the back of them but because leaving is the sign that things have gone well: the child has been sufficiently loved to be able to separate confidently.

In the ideal future, we'd have a culture that took an educational approach to relationships. It would have high ambitions around what a couple could teach one another and how they could grow through being together. But it would, consequently, see this as – in some cases – a finite task, as something that one could get done in a given span. The ideal duration of some people's relationship might be a month or five years or three decades. Breaking up wouldn't have to be a mark of failure; it could be a recognition that the good, essential work of sharing what each person had to offer the other had been completed. A relationship would finish not because it had failed but because it had royally succeeded.

21.

The Fear of Being Alone

One of the most important preconditions of a good relationship is a satisfactory perspective on being single. The more we are happy to be on our own, the more we will be able to exercise the correct degree of caution around finding a new companion. The bedrock of true love is happy singledom.

Unfortunately, our societies do very little to help us to be calm or at ease in our own company. Singledom is framed as an involuntary, depressing and always hopefully temporary state. The notion that someone might want or need to be on their own, perhaps for a long while, terrifies a world shaped by legions of silently miserable couples who need confirmation that they have not chosen the wrong path. To enforce the idea of what single people are missing, advertisers can never have enough of showing off tantalising images of happy couples walking hand in hand on beaches – and most entertainment venues, holiday destinations and social occasions feel compelled to patronise, overcharge and otherwise demean anyone who has had the impudence to venture out on their own.

Unfortunately, being miserable while single fatally undermines our judgement about who we might get together with. When someone is starving, they will eat anything, and we're equally liable, in emotional desperation, to run into the nearest nightclub to secure a chump we'll be appalled to find beside us at daybreak. We eventually learn that being in an unsatisfactory relationship is clearly worse – that is, even more lonely – than being alone.

The central challenge of being alone is coping with the fear of what singlehood *means*. We can begin with a simple observation: it's typically a lot worse to be on our own on a Saturday than on a Monday night, and a lot worse to be alone over the festive period than to be alone at the end of the tax year. The physical reality and the length of time we're by ourselves may be identical, but the feeling that comes with being so is entirely different. This apparently negligible observation holds out a clue for a substantial solution to loneliness. The difference between the Saturday and the Monday night comes down to the contrast between what being alone appears to *mean* on the two respective dates. On a Monday night, our own company feels like it brings no judgement in its wake; it doesn't in any way depart from the norms of respectable society; it's what's expected of decent people at the start of a busy week: we get back from work, make some soup, catch up on the post, do some emails and order a few groceries without any sense of being unusual or cursed. The next day, when a colleague asks us what we got up to, we can relate the truth without any hot prickles of shame. It was – after all – just a Monday night. But Saturday night finds us in a far more perilous psychological zone: we scan our phone for any sign of a last-minute invitation, we flick through the channels in an impatient and disconsolate haze, we are alive to our own tragedy as we eat tuna from a tin, we take a long bath at 8.30 p.m. to try to numb the discomfort inside with scalding heat on the outside, and as we prepare to turn out the light just after ten, the high-spirited cries of revellers walking by our house seem to convey a targeted tone of mockery and pity. On Monday morning, we pass over the whole horrid incident with haste.

From this we conclude: being alone is bearable in relation to how 'normal' (that highly nebulous yet highly influential concept) the condition feels to us at any given point; it can either be a break from an honourably busy life, or sure evidence that we are an unwanted, wretched, disgusting and emotionally diseased being.

This is tricky but ultimately very hopeful, for it suggests that if only we could work on what being alone means to us, we could theoretically end up as comfortable in our own skin on a long summer Saturday night filled with the joyous cries of our fellow citizens as on the dreariest Monday in November, and we could spend the whole holiday season by ourselves feeling as relaxed and as unselfconscious as we did when we were a child and hung out for days by ourselves, tinkering with a project on the floor of our bedroom, with no thought in the world that anyone would think us sad or shameful as a result. We may not – after all – need a new companion (something that can be hard to find in a panic); we just need a new mindset (which we can take care of by ourselves, starting right now).

To build ourselves a new mental model of what being alone should truly mean, we might rehearse a few of the following arguments. Despite what an unfriendly voice inside our heads might tell us, we are the ones who can choose whether or not to be alone. Our solitude is willed rather than imposed. No one ever needs to be alone so long as they don't mind who they are with. But we do mind: the wrong kind of company is a great deal lonelier for us than being by ourselves – that is, it's further from what matters to us, more grating in its insincerity and more of a reminder of disconnection and misunderstanding than is the conversation we can have in the quiet of our own minds. Being alone is not proof that we have been rejected by the world; it's a sign that we've taken a good look at the available options and have – with wisdom – done some rejecting ourselves.

It can of course, from a distance, sometimes seem as if everyone is having an ecstatic time. But we need to hold on to what we recognise in our sober moments as a more complicated reality: that there is going to be alienation at the restaurant, bitterness in couples and despair in sunny island hotels. Isolation and grief are not unique to us; they are a fundamental part of the human experience, they trail every member of our species, whether in couples or alone; we've chosen to experience the pains of existence by ourselves for now, but having a partner has never protected anyone from the void for very long. We should take care to drown our own individual sorrows in the ocean of a redemptive and darkly funny universal pessimism.

Another big thought is that we need to appreciate how long it will take to find someone, given how choosy we are (for very good reasons). We aren't just looking for anyone. The right candidate will be no less easy to find than a great job or a beautiful house. It might take many months, probably years. Expectations matter. If we regard a decade as a plausible time frame, then six months will skip by.

There is no better guarantee of a successful relationship than knowing that we could, and can, manage perfectly well on our own. It means that we will only look for someone who can deeply contribute to our life, not someone who can do the laundry with us or keep us company on Sunday evenings. This gives us the strength to back out of unsatisfactory unions as quickly as we should. Being in a couple can't and shouldn't mean that we are utterly reliant on the other for our self-esteem, our daily self-management or the meeting of our domestic needs. When we have under our belt a significant experience of thriving on our own, we will be able to cope with the inevitable points at which even a very nice partner can't sustain us; we'll be less demanding, more competent and more forensic in what we seek from a lover. It turns out that our willingness to stay on our own is what centrally predicts how likely we'll be to find and bring to fruition a relationship with someone else. Being at ease with being single is the needed, secure platform from which to make a sane and wise choice about who to create a joint life with.

22.

The Importance of Bad Dates

While waiting to find our life partner, we may end up going on a number of dates – and we stand to return from many of them in an incensed and depressed mood. Could such people really exist? What is wrong with the human race?

But a bad date doesn't have to be any sort of conclusive failure; if handled correctly, it may indeed be a crucial educational stage that underpins our chances of subsequent contentment. Apparently dreadful encounters can be among the most helpful experiences we ever pass through because they teach us two ingredients crucial to the maintenance of love: gratitude and realism.

In order to be grateful for the singular individual we end up with, we have to acquire an accurate sense of who and what is typical. If we have no idea how widespread a dry sense of humour is, or an analytical temper, or an empathetic nature, or a very kind heart, we'll be in no fair position to evaluate any person we eventually land on. We'll be like a wealthy young heir who has no way of knowing whether flying to Barbados in January is in any way more or less special than dropping in on a five-course meal at the foot of Mount Kilimanjaro or having tea with their grandmother in a modest house in the suburbs. Distinctions and virtues will cease to stand out. The muscles of appreciation will atrophy.

But a series of terrible dating encounters firmly educates us in what can generally be expected from the members of our benighted race. It is extremely important to spend a series of evenings in a bar with yet another person who is keen to parade their achievements in order properly to appreciate the rare pleasures of someone with a mature sense of modesty. Several hours with another accomplished professional (with lovely hair and a winning smile) who isn't very interested in our life might have a lot to teach us about where along the hierarchy of qualities we place intelligently targeted curiosity. It may take several encounters with extreme wealth or beauty to show us what we actually make of these initially extremely enticing-sounding features.

Rather than dismiss bad dates quickly from our minds, as we are prone to do, we should embed them carefully in our memory and even put up a private shrine to them in a diary or on our phone. Every bad date will, in a covert form, contain clues as to the essence of satisfactory love. The one who turned up twenty minutes late without calling will harden our determination to cherish punctuality. The one who used cynicism to defend themselves against their own ambitions can teach us to appreciate an open-hearted sense of purpose. The one who was sexually driven but emotionally detached can serve as a lesson in the need for warmth and sympathy in any bedroom encounter. From the marks of failure we can discern the shape of success.

To sustain us with our partners, we need to keep brightly alive the many differences between them and the mass of humanity, whose nature we will have had a chance to surmise in the slow and troubled years before they appeared. We will know that our partner is not perfect, but – thanks to a litany of bad dates – we will also understand exactly where they slot into the spectrum of compromise, muddle and error. We will – with any luck – know to be very grateful.

By keeping our dating adventures firmly in mind, we are reminding ourselves that plenty of people may look fascinating from the outset but will in fact prove hopeless for us in the long term. Properly digested failure immunises us forever against that particular cancer of relationships: the idea that someone else, somewhere else, would surely be better. The nebulous pull of the alluring stranger can weaken. We will be a little less prone to developing crushes on imaginary figments and a little readier to invest in the all-too-human and well-charted person beside us.

Conclusion

We've been unpacking a range of possible responses to some of the problems of love. We hope this book might be consulted at varied moments of difficulty and confusion – perhaps late at night, after a long argument in the kitchen, or on a train journey home, when everything has grown bleak and confusing.

When we suffer from ...	We might turn to ...
A mood of defensiveness in the couple	Chapter 1
A temptation to have an affair	Chapter 18
Low self-esteem	Chapter 3
Detachment and resentment	Chapter 15

But, inevitably, there will be times when we'll encounter problems to which no specific solutions are mentioned here, and it's for these occasions that we end with a few more general thoughts to attenuate our sadness and alleviate our puzzlement.

Happiness is cyclical

We know the lesson well enough in relation to the seasons: autumn will follow summer; balmy evenings need to give way to bitter winds. In love, we long so much for eternally clear skies, but there can be no avoiding periods of harshness and reversal. The very desire to get married is, in a sense, born of a wish to be content *forever*. Yet nothing human is capable of such endurance and stability. We are creatures mostly made of water; our vows can only ever be aspirations written in air, rather than guarantees chiselled in marble.

Inevitably, therefore, we will hit problems – serious ones, too, at risk of being made all the worse by our innocence. Last week everything might have appeared masterable. We were looking forward to the future; we couldn't imagine not delighting in one another. And yet we're in difficulties again. Someone is angry about something; someone isn't sure any more. There was shouting and even some very horrid insults. We can't even quite remember the sequence, but we know well enough the moods of resentment, suspicion and scratchiness in which we are now mired.

We should take comfort from knowing that, as sure as this storm descended on us, so it will lift. Our challenges are those of every human who has ever tried to tie themselves intimately to another. We are suffering under no undue curse; we are just trying to do something very difficult.

Awe at the complexity

The more we have imbibed an impression that a good relationship is a birthright, the more we will be catapulted into frustration by whatever struggles we encounter. And yet the more we can have faith that this is – at times, by necessity – a nightmare for everyone, the more we will be kind to ourselves and our maddening partners and may, eventually, laugh. We need not compound our problems by believing that they are – on top of everything else – unusual. They are par for the course. We are stumbling around, lost and furious, hurt and sad, exactly the way we are meant to. There was never going to be an alternative. Our problems aren't a sign that we have made a mistake; they're evidence that we're properly engaging with the process. This is love. The songs and the movies have got it very wrong. Only a few books will ever dare to whisper how it is.

A serious relationship is an attempt by two people to be happy together forever. Simply rereading that sentence should make us laugh (sometimes scream). If there were a god above able to listen to our blather, they would guffaw or send us a few hurricanes to tame our hubris. What cosmic impudence! What profound misunderstanding of the material of which we're made! Most of us can't manage fifteen minutes of satisfaction on our own; and somehow we have managed to hallucinate that we might double up and bank forty-five years of contentment side by side, perhaps with two children, a dog, a cramped home, a busy career and a range of ever-increasing physical ailments. We are truly being very nasty to ourselves.

We would have a lot more reason to smile if only we could be more pessimistic. There should be lessons in melancholy about love in primary school. We assess how we're doing at any task relative to an overarching sense of how complex it might be. If we think a journey should take half an hour, we go half wild with frustration when we're still only at the starting gate at lunchtime, but if we imagine the trip will take an entire day, maybe two, we'll be delighted by the incremental progress we're making. An ideally wise society would constantly correctly signpost the arduousness of love: a relationship would be framed as the almost impossible task of coordinating the emotional and practical existences of two necessarily insane individuals of different backgrounds, tastes, ways of thinking and patterns of feeling, both attempting to grasp for satisfaction against the mutual clash of their complex histories and the ticking of the clock towards painful eternal demise.

There will be no way this will ever go smoothly just because we have (at key moments) been very fond of one another. Wedding speeches should resemble send-offs for adventurers about to cross Antarctica or colonise Mars; ritual wailing and lamentation would most rightly accompany all announcements of marriage.

There will be complications everywhere

If we had been properly forewarned, we would know how practically anything – however innocent it might seem – may turn into grounds for misery. And so we would be a lot less panicky around the horrors we did run into. Three days of sulking? Of course. A threat of divorce? Naturally. An affair (on both sides)? Why not? We would – with resignation and something close to dark glee – be expecting something ghastly every new day.

Maybe a difficult clash of opinions could emerge around car insurance or how much bottled water it is appropriate to drink. A walk to the shops might unleash an episode of resentment about who should be responsible for the heavier bag. There might be an argument about what it means to brush one's teeth *for too long*.

We'd imagine that a weekend away together would probably involve a row, a hotel that was not quite as nice as it looked in the photos, a dinner with awkward stretches of silence between us – but maybe also, hopefully, an afternoon walk when we really did talk properly and just maybe (but perhaps not) a drowsy, comfortable morning in bed together.

Gratitude

With such darkness in mind, we would be readier to bless our fortunes in whatever increments they came. If we had spent a pleasant afternoon together, we would know to say thank you. We'd take nothing for granted about a five-day break that had unfolded without crisis. We would think we were doing well if we could celebrate our second anniversary and still want to make love or like getting home early to spend extra time in the beloved's arms. What immense good fortune to be calling them 'sweet pea' or 'baby lamb' after a decade. A genuinely considerate comment would become something precious; an apology that was properly meant would be a triumph (even if we knew the same problem would doubtless resurface before long).

As part of this gratitude, we'd do a lot more investigating; every sigh would get attention. We wouldn't assume that a partner wasn't planning an affair or a chat with a divorce lawyer. We'd regularly ask them if they were angry with us or wanted something else – and would listen very carefully to the answers. We'd repeatedly apologise for existing – and hope that they would, with equal humility, do much the same.

Laughter

To lie like this would mean to laugh a lot more often. There are good reasons why an ability to laugh is one of the most sought-after qualities in a prospective partner. It's not idle japes we're looking for. We want, first and foremost, someone who can laugh at *themselves*, someone who can see their own ridiculousness and admit to it with grace. And we need to do likewise.

Laughter occupies the zone between our hopes and the available reality. It is the best possible response to the difference between the way we want things to be and the complicated way they actually are. To make a joke, all we ever need to do is to look at one of our hopes and compare it with what life has truly delivered. I wanted to be happy forever, *then I met your parents*. I used to think I was easy going, *then I opened one of your cupboards*. I thought people who strayed were evil, *then I swore to be eternally faithful*. We can add in entries ad infinitum.

How we wanted it to be	How it has turned out

Love

And yet, despite everything, this is a book about love. Which means, first and foremost, this is a book about forgiveness, charity and the need to display ongoing kindness towards ourselves and others for the difficulty and foolishness involved in being human.

We would – naturally – have every right to be furious about how things often end up in relationships. But to commit ourselves to love involves an almost arbitrary decision to approach matters in another way: no longer as an angry customer whose guarantees and promises have been betrayed, but as a parent looking at their wilful, very naughty and only intermittently sane child, knowing that whatever the chaos and the challenge, love will go on.

Every time we confront a problem, we can at least be assured that there is a chance to learn. Beneath any conflict is something we have not yet mastered. We are in pain again, but we have been granted another opportunity to be curious and to take a lesson at an establishment we are bittersweetly never quite done with: the school of love.

To join The School of Life community and find out more,
scan below:

The School of Life publishes a range of books on essential topics
in psychological and emotional life, including relationships,
parenting, friendship, careers and fulfilment. The aim is always
to help us to understand ourselves better and thereby to grow
calmer, less confused and more purposeful. Discover our full
range of titles, including books for children, here:
www.theschooloflife.com/books

The School of Life also offers a comprehensive therapy service,
which complements, and draws upon, our published works:
www.theschooloflife.com/therapy